DRAYTON HALL
An Annotated Bibliography

RESEARCH ON HISTORIC PROPERTIES
OCCASIONAL PAPERS: NO 2

Compiled by William Bynum

The Preservation Press
National Trust for Historic Preservation in the United States

Drayton Hall: An Annotated Bibliography is the second in a series of research reports from the Office of Historic Properties of the National Trust for Historic Preservation. These reports present studies pertaining to various aspects of preservation and research on the structures, sites and collections maintained by the National Trust.

The National Trust for Historic Preservation, chartered by Congress in 1949, is the only private, nonprofit organization with the responsibility to encourage public participation in the preservation of sites, buildings and objects significant in American history and culture. Support is provided by membership dues, endowment funds and contributions and by matching grants from federal agencies, including the U.S. Department of the Interior, Heritage Conservation and Recreation Service, under provisions of the National Historic Preservation Act of 1966.

THE PRESERVATION PRESS
National Trust for Historic Preservation
740-748 Jackson Place, N.W.
Washington, D.C. 20006

Cover: Historic American Buildings Survey measured drawing of Drayton Hall.
Title page: Photograph of Drayton Hall land facade by Louis Schwartz, 1973.

CONTENTS

Drayton Hall on the Ashley River northwest of Charleston, S.C., is a manifestation of the plantation system that brought wealth, culture and grandeur to the South Carolina low country in the 18th and 19th centuries. Built between 1738 and 1742, Drayton Hall was the country seat of the Hon. John Drayton and was held by seven generations of his family until 1974.

For two centuries this finest surviving example of early Georgian architecture in the South has been a source of enjoyment and intrigue for scholars and casual visitors alike. When John Drayton built his home only seven decades had passed since 1670, the year of the first permanent settlement by Europeans in South Carolina. The importance of the dwelling derives from the sophistication at such an early date of its design, incorporating a two-story Palladian portico and two flanking dependencies. The rich ornamentation of the interior enhances the building's significance. Despite much research the name of the architect or the master builder remains unknown.

The building has survived in almost unblemished condition despite war (the American Revolution and especially the War Between the States when all other houses on the west bank of the Ashley were burned by Federal troops), hurricanes, the great earthquake of 1886 and the economic pressures of the 20th century. Drayton Hall has never been modernized with gas lights, electricity, plumbing or any heating system other than its 13 original fireplaces.

Although Drayton Hall was unoccupied for long periods after the War Between the States, it suffered only minor damage. By the second half of this century, however, the Drayton family realized they would have to find another owner to assure the estate's survival. This was accomplished by a unique and innovative arrangement. The National Trust for Historic Preservation and Historic Charleston Foundation took a lease option in 1973 to purchase the property. By late 1974 funds for the purchase had been raised with assistance from the South Carolina Department of Parks, Recreation & Tourism and two agencies of the U.S. Department of the Interior--the Bureau of Outdoor Recreation and the National Park Service. Drayton Hall is jointly owned by the National Trust and the state of South Carolina and is operated with the advice of Historic Charleston Foundation, an arrangement that may serve as a prototype for new approaches to the management of historic sites.

Since purchase of the property in 1974, the National Trust has assigned staff to Drayton Hall to do research and necessary maintenance while at the same time it opened the property to National Trust members and the public on a limited basis. At the beginning of 1978 visiting was expanded at the property to seven days a week.

The first research project was an exploration of the property by the Trust archaeologist, carried out over a period of 21 months. Next, an architect and an architectural historian studied the house for 15 months. Their work included excavations, measured drawings, wood and paint analyses, a structural stress load study, moisture content, interior x-raying, documentary research and other necessary investigations.

Drayton Hall: An Annotated Bibliography is the first Drayton Hall research
report to be published and is designed to further research on the estate.
William Bynum, a graduate student at the University of Virginia, conducted
an exhaustive survey, accomplished in 10 weeks, of material on Drayton Hall
and the Drayton family in four repositories in Charleston.

This report is indicative of the cooperative development of Drayton Hall.
The author's research was funded jointly by the National Trust and the state
of South Carolina through its Governor's Intern Program. Sincere appreciation
is extended to Gov. James B. Edwards and Kathleen C. Cecil, program coordina-
tor, for assistance in this effort and in continuing joint projects. Gale
S. Alder, National Trust architectural historian, aided in the conception,
administration and publication of the report and Barbara Hurlbutt, associate
editor for the National Trust, worked within very strict time limitations
to prepare the report for publication. Thanks are extended to the staffs of
the repositories where the author did his research and which he mentions in
the preface to this report. Our deep appreciation goes to Miss Sally Reahard,
a devoted friend of Drayton Hall, for her earlier bibliography, which was
helpful in the formulation of this work.

Research at Drayton Hall will never be completed. The availability and use
of this annotated bibliography should be an effective tool in aiding further
work.

Dennis T. Lawson, administrator, Drayton Hall

This bibliography is the result of a research project undertaken during the period June - August 1977. All material available on Drayton Hall and the Drayton family in the collections of the South Carolina Historical Society, Charleston Library Society, Charleston County Public Library and the Robert S. Small Library of the College of Charleston was examined.

The bibliography includes all significant material on the Drayton family and Drayton Hall available at these institutions, with the exception of the collections at the South Carolina Historical Society, which are not indexed in the main card catalogue there. (The Drayton family papers owned by Historic Charleston Foundation were being organized and stabilized in Columbia during the period of research and were not available.)

For purposes of scholarship, this bibliography is in two parts: Part I consists of works having a direct reference to Drayton Hall or the Drayton family, while Part II consists of materials that do not refer to either Drayton Hall or the Drayton family but provide useful background information on life in the South Carolina low country and the plantation system. The photographs are included as illustrative material only and were not collected as part of the project. Therefore, not all can be found in the four repositories searched.

My thanks go to Margueretta Childs, archivist of the College of Charleston; Virginia Rugheimer and the staff of the Charleston Library Society; Gene Waddell, Sallie Doscher and other staff members of the South Carolina Historical Society. Special thanks to Dennis T. Lawson, National Trust administrator of Drayton Hall, whose encouragement and advice have been most valuable, and to Janet McNeill, then secretary at Drayton Hall, who was willing to type even last-minute changes from scribbled notes.

William Bynum, research assistant, Drayton Hall, under South
       Carolina Governor's Intern Program, 1977

DRAYTON HALL: AN ANNOTATED BIBLIOGRAPHY

PART I

MATERIALS HAVING A DIRECT REFERENCE
TO DRAYTON HALL OR THE DRAYTON FAMILY

BOOKS

American Heritage. The American Heritage History of Notable American Houses.
    New York: American Heritage Publishing Co., 1971. CLS

    Quotation from Gov. John Drayton on South Carolina houses and gardens
    (p. 67). Brief description of Drayton Hall and photograph of land front
    (p. 73).

Andrews, Wayne. Architecture, Ambition and Americans. New York: Harper
    & Brothers, 1947. CC, CCPL, CLS

    Praise of Drayton Hall (p. 26); photograph of land front (p. 27); way of
    life of the South Carolina upper class (pp. 24, 25, 33).

    Errata: "The Hon. John Drayton, a Barbadian immigrant." John was not
    an immigrant, his father (or, possibly, his grandfather) was. "William
    Drayton, Chief Justice of the colony." He was chief justice of East
    Florida, not South Carolina.

Architects' Emergency Committee. Great Georgian Houses in America. Vol. 1
    New York: Architects' Emergency Committee, 1933. CC, CCPL, CLS

    Drayton Hall; photograph of land front (p. 24). Plan of Drayton Hall,
    elevation of land front and of walls in the Great Hall (pp. 25-29).
    Foreword mentions a number of architectural books used in the colonies
    (pp. 9-19). Charleston houses (pp. 30-45).

Baldwin, Agnes Leland. First Settlers of South Carolina, 1670-80. Columbia:
    University of South Carolina Press for the South Carolina Tricentennial
    Commission, 1969. CCPL, CLS, SCHS

    Thomas Drayton mentioned in list of settlers--his property, occupation,

---

Key to repositories where materials may be found:
    CC   - College of Charleston
    CCPL - Charleston County Public Library
    CLS - Charleston Library Society
    SCHS - South Carolina Historical Society

I. BOOKS

origin and arrival in 1679.

Ball, William Watts. _The State That Forgot: South Carolina's Surrender to Democracy_. Indianapolis: Bobbs-Merrill, 1932. CC, CCPL, CLS, SCHS

Deals with the aristocratic tradition and its decline in South Carolina politics. Brief mentions of William Henry Drayton (p. 40), Gov. John Drayton (p. 51).

Bass, Robert D. _Gamecock: The Life and Campaigns of General Thomas Sumter_. New York: Holt, Rinehart and Winston, 1961. CC, CCPL, CLS

Mentions William Henry Drayton's political activities early in the Revolution (pp. 25-31). Brief mention of Governor John Drayton, 1810 (p. 244).

Boucher, Chauncey Samuel. _The Nullification Controversy in South Carolina_. Chicago: University of Chicago Press, 1916. CC, CLS, CCPL

Deals extensively with Col. William Drayton's efforts to retain the Union, 1830-33.

Bowes, Frederick P. _The Culture of Early Charleston_. Chapel Hill: University of North Carolina Press, 1942. CC, CCPL, CLS, SCHS

A survey of religion, education, literature, science and art in the colonial low country. Mention of Charles Drayton (pp. 77-78), William Drayton (p. 123), William Henry Drayton (pp. 127-28). Gov. John Drayton quoted on South Carolinians' fondness for everything British (p. 93).

Briggs, Loutrel. _Charleston Gardens_. Columbia: University of South Carolina Press, 1951. CC, CCPL, CLS, SCHS

Same information as in Lockwood (see Books, Part I). Plans of gardens no longer in existence at various plantations (pp.104-12). Drayton Hall gardens (p. 105).

Bull, Henry de Saussure. _The Family of Stephen Bull_. Georgetown, S.C.: Winyah Press, 1961. CCPL, CLS, SCHS

Genealogy of descendants of John Drayton and Charlotta Bull (William Henry and Charles Drayton) traced (pp. 63-75).

Burton, E. Milby. _Charleston Furniture 1700-1825_. Columbia: University of South Carolina Press, 1970. CC, CLS, SCHS

Important information on Charleston-made furniture, although none specifically on Drayton Hall furnishings, much of which was apparently made in Charleston. (See Elfe, Magazines and Journals, Part I) Gov. John Drayton's sales of two lots on New Street mentioned (p. 116).

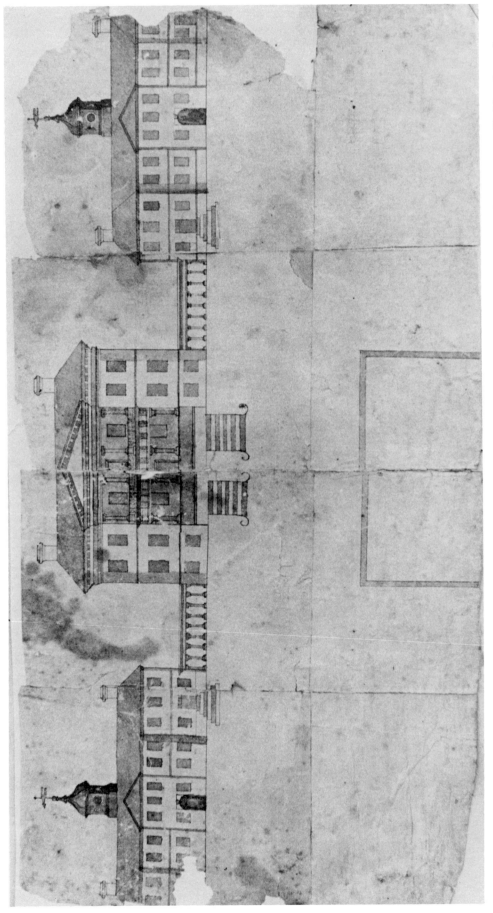

Figure 1: Anonymous drawing, date unknown, found among Drayton family papers. Although Drayton Hall closely resembles the design of the central structure, the flanking brick buildings actually constructed at Drayton Hall
differed greatly from those depicted in the drawing. (Courtesy of Historic Charleston Foundation)

I. BOOKS

_____. _The Siege of Charleston 1861-1865_. Columbia: University of South Carolina Press, 1970. CC, CCPL, CLS, SCHS

References to the Drayton brothers: Thomas F., Confederate general; Percival, Union Navy officer (pp. 75, 90, 137).

Cardozo, Jacob N. _Reminiscences of Charleston_. Charleston: Joseph Walker, 1866. CC, CCPL, CLS, SCHS

Deals mainly with Charleston area during the War Between the States. Brief mention of Gen. Thomas Drayton (p. 83).

Chamberlain, Samuel, and Narcissa Chamberlain. _Southern Interiors of Charleston, South Carolina_. New York: Hastings House, 1956. CC, CCPL, CLS, SCHS

Photographs of interiors of Charleston-area houses. Photographs showing furniture originally at Drayton Hall, now at the Heyward-Washington House (pp. 45-46). Photographs showing silver service and chessmen once owned by John Grimke Drayton of Magnolia (pp. 113-14). "Drayton Hall... is very probably the finest untouched example of Georgian architecture still standing in America. It has survived the years unblemished by gas, electricity or central heating" (pp. 158-63).

Errata: "Some of the original paint actually remains on its beautifully paneled walls." All rooms have been painted at least twice, according to the National Trust for Historic Preservation architectural study. "[The Great Hall's] plaster ceiling centerpiece...has remained intact for more than two centuries." The present ceiling of the great hall dates from around 1860.

Uncorroborated statements: "The original plan included two extensive wings..." An anonymous design showing such wings exists, but it is not certain that the design is indeed of Drayton Hall. The house, as built, included flankers, but they were relatively small and plain. "In 1865, Drayton Hall had providentially been turned into a hospital." This is a traditional but undocumented statement.

Charleston Chamber of Commerce. _Historic and Picturesque Charleston, South Carolina_. Charleston: Walker, Evans and Cogswell, 1904. CCPL

Like most sources that give a specific date, this book claims that the house "was built in 1740." The book repeats the questionable story that the house was Cornwallis's headquarters "for a time" (p. 20).

Charleston Old and New, and its Francis Marion Hotel. [Charleston: 193?]. SCHS

A promotional guidebook including a brief statement on "Drayton Hall and

Phosphate Mines."

Erratum: "The property had been in the family since 1671." Actually 1738.

Charleston, South Carolina in 1883. Boston: Heliotype Printing Co., 1883. CLS, SCHS

Guidebook with numerous photographs (none of Drayton Hall). "For some years after the late war it [Drayton Hall] was uninhabited, but is now occupied, and no longer open to tourists" (pp. 38-39).

Errata: " 'Drayton Hall' which was built in 1746 (of bricks imported from England), by John Drayton, Esq., after the style of Drayton Manor, in Northamptonshire, the home of his grandfather, who came with Sir John Yeamans to Carolina in 1671, and settled upon tracts known as Drayton Hall and Magnolia." Probably the bricks were locally made. Drayton Manor in Northamptonshire is a medieval building bearing no resemblance to Drayton Hall; John Drayton's grandfather (according to some sources, his father) probably came from Barbados in 1679, and long after Drayton Manor had passed from the hands of the Draytons. He never owned the Drayton Hall property, which John Drayton bought in 1738.

Uncorroborated statement: "Drayton Hall was for some time the headquarters of Cornwallis." It is not known that Cornwallis was at Drayton Hall for more than a day, and at the time he was second in command to Sir Henry Clinton. (See Uhlendorf, Books, Part I, and Clinton and Wilson, Magazines and Journals, Part I)

Chazal, Philip E. The Century in Phosphates and Fertilizers. Charleston: Lucas & Richardson, 1904. CLS, CCPL, SCHS

History and chemistry of the South Carolina phosphate industry. "Drayton Mines, Ashley River" (p. 62) listed among the phosphate mines.

Chesnut, Mary Boykin. A Diary from Dixie. Edited by Isabella D. Martin and Myrta L. Avery. New York: D. Appleton & Co., 1905. CC, CLS, CCPL, SCHS. Second edition edited by Ben Ames Williams. Houghton Mifflin Co., 1949.

Life in Charleston, Montgomery and Richmond during the War Between the States as viewed by a general's wife. Many valuable insights into the feelings and doubts of the Confederate "aristocracy" concerning their way of life and conduct of the war.

Mention of "Tom" (Gen. Thomas F.) Drayton (great-grandnephew of John, Drayton Hall builder) (p. 148).

I. BOOKS

Coats, Peter. <u>Great Gardens of the Western World</u>. New York: G.P. Putnam's Sons, 1963. CLS

Description of John Grimke Drayton's Magnolia Gardens (pp. 189-90).

Cohen, Hennig. <u>The South Carolina Gazette 1732-1775</u>. Columbia: University of South Carolina Press, 1953. CC, CCPL, CLS, SCHS

Survey of most areas of social and cultural life in South Carolina, 1732-1775, illustrated by extracts from the <u>South-Carolina Gazette</u>. Several brief mentions of Charles and William Henry Drayton. Lists architects, engineers, master builders, architectural books, gardening and gardeners mentioned in the <u>Gazette</u> (pp. 58-70).

<u>Cyclopedia of Eminent and Representative Men of the Carolinas of the Nineteenth Century</u>. 2 vols. Madison, Wis.: Brant & Fuller, 1892; reprinted, Spartanburg, S.C.: The Reprint Co., 1972. CC, CCPL, CLS, SCHS

Biographical sketch of Gov. John Drayton (vol. 1, pp. 263-64).

Dabney, William M., and Dargan, Marion. <u>William Henry Drayton and the American Revolution</u>. Albuquerque: University of New Mexico Press, 1962. SCHS, CLS, CC

A study of South Carolina during the Revolutionary period and a biography of William Henry Drayton, the most complete source of information on him included in this bibliography. Appendix gives text of his two best-known speeches. Several mentions of other Draytons.

Davidson, Chalmers Gaston. <u>The Last Foray: The South Carolina Planters of 1860</u>. Columbia: University of South Carolina Press, 1971. CC, CCPL, CLS, SCHS

A "sociological study" of the characteristics of the largest planters in 1860. Thomas Fenwick Drayton's branch of the family had surpassed the older branch in wealth (pp. 3-4); Thomas Fenwick Drayton mentioned (pp. 38, 148); biographical sketch of him (p. 192). The Drayton Hall branch not included because of the author's arbitrary limitation of the study to families owning "100 or more slaves in a single district or parish."

Davis, Evangeline. <u>Charleston Houses and Gardens</u>. Charleston: Preservation Society of Charleston, 1975. CCPL, CLS, SCHS

An unpaginated collection of photographs and captions, including one of Drayton Hall.

Davis, John. <u>Travels of Four Years and a Half in the United States of America</u>. London: 1803. CC, CLS, SCHS

Davis spent more than a year as tutor in the family of Thomas Drayton
(son of John, Drayton Hall builder). Illustrates "elegance" of the family lifestyle at the end of the 18th century. Life at Ocean Plantation
near Coosawhatchie: hunting, slaves, climate (pp. 67-101); life at
Magnolia and in Charleston (pp. 102-112); "An elder brother of Mr. Drayton
[Dr. Charles Drayton] was our neighbour on the river; he occupied, perhaps, the largest house [Drayton Hall] and gardens in the United States
of America" (p. 106).

Dictionary of American Biography. Biographical sketches of notable members
of the Drayton family. Note: the John Drayton listed here is not the
builder of Drayton Hall but his grandson who became governor of South
Carolina. "Drayton, John," "Drayton, William" (1732-1790), "Drayton,
William" (1776-1846), by James H. Easterby and Dumas Malone; "Drayton,
Thomas Fenwick," by James H. Easterby; "Drayton, Percival," by Charles
O. Paullin; and "Drayton, William Henry," by Marion Dargan. CC (1964 ed.),
CCPL (1956 ed.)

Drayton, John. The Carolinian Florist of Governor John Drayton of South
Carolina. Edited by Margaret Babcock Meriwether. Columbia: South
Caroliniana Library, 1943. CC, CCPL, CLS, SCHS

A survey of South Carolina plants written in 1807 by a grandson of John,
Drayton Hall builder. This edition includes the author's history of the
Drayton family (pp.xxiii-xxxiv). (See also Drayton, J.[Gov.] Manuscripts,
Part I.)

Drayton, John. Memoirs of the American Revolution, from Its Commencement to
the Year 1776, Inclusive; as Relating to the State of South-Carolina:
and Occasionally Referring to the States of North-Carolina and Georgia.
2 vols. Charleston: A.E. Miller, 1821; reprinted, New York: Arno Press,
1969. CC, CCPL, CLS, SCHS

Edited manuscripts and papers of William Henry Drayton, son of John,
Drayton Hall builder. Biographical sketch of William Henry Drayton
(vol. 1, pp. xiii-xxvii). Both volumes illustrate William Henry Drayton's
leadership in the Revolutionary War movement from 1773 to 1776.

Erratum: "He was the eldest son of John Drayton," (p. xiii). Actually
the eldest surviving son.

Uncorroborated statement: "Thomas Drayton...came to South-Carolina...in
the year 1671." A Thomas Drayton arrived in 1679; there is no documentation for any earlier arrival.

Drayton, John. A View of South-Carolina; As Respects Her Natural and Civil
Concerns. Charleston: W.P. Young, 1802. CC, CCPL, CLS, SCHS

General description of gardens on the Ashley River: "And here elegant
buildings arose, which overlooked grounds, where art and nature were

Figure 2: Staircase, first floor stair hall, ca. 1937. (Frances Benjamin Johnston photograph, Library of Congress)

happily combined. Gardeners were imported from Europe; and soon the
stately laurel [magnolia], and the soft spreading elm, shot up their
heads in avenues and walks: while they were occasionally clasped by
the yellow jasmine, or crimson wood-bine. Soon the verdant lawn spread
forth its carpet, contrasted with hedges, gravel walks, terraces, and
wildernesses" (p. 112). Descriptions of the vegetation, climate, dis-
eases, etc. of low country South Carolina (pp. 6-30); houses and gardens
(pp. 111-112); agriculture (pp. 112-144); slavery, with proslavery argu-
ments (pp. 188-189); miscellaneous information on Charleston (pp. 200-
206); education and "Modes of Living" (fashion, social classes, etc.)
(pp. 217-227).

Drayton, William. The Farewell Address of the Hon. William Drayton, to the
    Washington Society (printed along with Grimke, Thomas S., Oration on the
    Principal Duties of Americans). Charleston: William Estill, 1833. CLS

Defense of the Union by Drayton (grandnephew of the Hon. John Drayton)
before moving from Charleston to Philadelphia.

Drayton, William. An Oration Delivered in the First Presbyterian Church,
    Charleston, Monday, July 4, 1831: to which is Annexed an Account of
    the Celebration of the 55th Anniversary of American Independence, by
    the Union and State Rights Party. Charleston: William S. Blain & James
    S. Burges, 1831. SCHS

Opposes nullification of tariff because it is a threat to the U.S.
Constitution and a step toward civil war.

Edgar, Walter B., ed. Biographical Directory of the South Carolina House of
    Representatives. Vol. 1. Columbia: University of South Carolina Press,
    1974. CC, CLS

Lists of members from each district in various sessions of the South
Carolina lower house from the colonial period to the 1970s. Good source
of basic information on the political service of the Draytons.

Enslow, J. Dean. The Resources and Attractions of Charleston, S.C. Charles-
    ton: Lucas & Richardson Co., [ca. 1898]. SCHS

"Drayton Hall, the only remaining one of these old homes in this immediate section, was built by Thomas Drayton, in 1740. This house was
occupied by Cornwallis as his headquarters in 1780 and 1781. The building was spared during the late war on account of its occupancy as a
hospital, and under the erroneous supposition that its owner was a
Unionist. This stately survival of colonial times has been completely
restored, and is the winter residence of Mr. Charles H. Drayton [IV],
2nd great-grandson of John, Drayton Hall builder. It is exceedingly
valuable on account of rich deposits of phosphates, which have been suc-
cessfully mined there for a number of years" (p. 48). Descriptions of
Magnolia Gardens and Middleton Place (p. 48).

I. BOOKS

Erratum: "built by Thomas Drayton" (actually John).

Uncorroborated statements: "...the only remaining one of these old homes."
It is believed that the house at Jeny's Plantation on the other side of
the Ashley River survived until it was burned in the early 1900s. "Occupied by Cornwallis as his headquarters in 1780 and 1781." Cornwallis
was in the Charleston area only for a few months in 1780, and no original
sources mention his being at Drayton Hall except on March 28-29, 1780.
(See Uhlendorf, Books, Part I and Clinton and Wilson, Magazines and
Journals, Part I) "The building was spared during the late war on account
of...." Both of these stories are widely repeated, but neither has been
substantiated.

Exchange Club of St. Andrew's Parish. The Progress of St. Andrew's Parish:
    1706-1947. [Charleston], 1947. CCPL, CLS

Not paginated. Includes the "legend" that Dr. John Drayton, "the owner,"
saved the house by claiming falsely that the slaves had smallpox.

Federal Writers' Project (Writers' Program of the Work Projects Administra-
    tion) South Carolina: A Guide to the Palmetto State. New York: Oxford
University Press, 1941. CLS

"Drayton Hall....The only Ashley River home not vandalized by Yankees in
1865, it was saved because a Confederate officer learned of the enemy ap-
proach and transferred a number of slaves, ill with smallpox into the
house" (p. 285). William Henry Drayton mentioned (pp. 32, 33, 100).

Fisher, Sidney George. Men, Women, and Manners in Colonial Times. 2 vols.
    Philadelphia: J.B. Lippincott Co., 1898. CC, CCPL

An informal "social" history of colonial America. Drayton Hall mentioned (vol. 2, p. 320).

Erratum: "[The plantation houses of S.C.?] were all destroyed in the
civil war except Drayton Hall, which, being used as a hospital, was
preserved, and is still shown to tourists and visitors from Charleston."
Many other plantations in the low country and other parts of the state
survived.

Fraser, Charles. Reminiscences of Charleston. Charleston: John Russell,
    1854. CC, CCPL, CLS, SCHS

Several mentions of Judge William Drayton in late 1700s and early 1800s.
Design of Charleston County Courthouse attributed to him.

Gibbes, R.W. Documentary History of the American Revolution. 3 vols. New
    York: D. Appleton & Co., 1855-57; reprinted, Spartanburg, S.C.: The
    Reprint Co., 1972. CC, CCPL, SCHS

Many references to William Henry Drayton, one reference to Thomas Drayton. (see indexes.)

Graydon, Nell S. _Eliza of Wappoo_. Columbia, S.C.: R.L. Bryan, 1967. CC, CCPL, CLS, SCHS

A semi-fictionalized biography of Eliza Lucas Pinckney, an influential plantation lady in 18th-century South Carolina. Description of dinner and ball at Drayton Hall, December 1743 (pp. 149-53). This passage is mostly fiction; for example, it mentions a reflecting pool near the house, but such a pool probably did not exist until circa 1900.

Guess, William Francis. _South Carolina: Annals of Pride and Protest_. New York: Harper & Bros., 1860. CC, CCPL, CLS, SCHS

Description of Charles Drayton's wedding celebration at Drayton Hall [1774] (pp. 59-60), largely from Ravenel, H.H.R. (see Books, Part I). Crops and slavery in the colony (pp. 60-63); life in colonial Charleston area (pp. 85-102). Mention of William Henry Drayton (pp. 110-17); Gov. John Drayton (p. 154).

Hamer, Philip M., et al., eds. _The Papers of Henry Laurens_. 5 vols. to date. Columbia: University of South Carolina Press, 1968-. CC, CLS, SCHS

Papers of a Charleston merchant aristocrat. Monetary transactions involving John Drayton, Drayton Hall builder, (vol. 1, p. 380; vol. 5, pp. 536, 552, 634). Ships owned by John and William Henry Drayton (vol. 5, 257n). Miscellaneous biographical information on William Henry, Thomas (brother of John), William (nephew of John, son of Thomas) and John Drayton (vol. 2, 166n, 380; vol. 5, 261 n, 536n).

Hamlin, Talbot Faulkner. _The American Spirit in Architecture_. New Haven: Yale University Press, 1926. CCPL

Brief description of Drayton Hall, one photograph (p. 85).

Hennig, Helen Kohn. _Great South Carolinians from Colonial Days to the Confederate War_. Chapel Hill: University of North Carolina Press, 1940. CCPL, CLS, SCHS

Written for young people. Biographical sketch of William Henry Drayton (pp. 125-39), has several errors about Drayton Hall, apparently based on Woolson (see Magazines and Journals, Part I) and Lathrop (see Books, Part I). For better information on W.H. Drayton, see Dabney and Dargan (Books, Part I).

Holmgren, Virginia C. _Hilton Head: A Sea Island Chronicle_. Hilton Head, S.C.: Hilton Head Publishing Co., 1959. CC, CCPL, CLS, SCHS

Gen. Thomas Drayton and Capt. Percival Drayton on opposite sides at the Battle of Port Royal (pp. 82-93). Story of Drayton land ownership on Hilton Head Island (p. 126). Note: Anna Drayton Stone's letter (see Manuscripts, Part I) claims that Holmgren's information on Drayton properties is inaccurate.

Hotten, John Camden, ed. <u>Our Early Emigrant Ancestors: The Original Lists...</u> <u>1600-1700.</u> (Cover title is <u>Lists of Emigrants to America 1600-1700.</u>) London: Chatto & Windus, 1874; reprinted, Baltimore: Genealogical Publishing Co., 1962. CCPL, CLS, SCHS

Lists of emigrants. Thomas Drayton, Jr., departure for Carolina, 1679 (p. 362). Rather modest property holdings of Thomas Drayton (possibly father of the Thomas, Jr., who came to Carolina) listed in Barbados census, circa 1679-80 (p. 453).

Johnson, John. <u>The Defense of Charleston Harbor.</u> Charleston: Walker, Evans & Cogswell Co., 1890; reprinted, Freeport, N.Y.: Books for Libraries Press, 1970. CC, CCPL, CLS, SCHS

Mention of Gen. Thomas F. Drayton at time of attack on the harbor, 7 April 1863 (pp. 45-60).

Johnson, Joseph. <u>Traditions and Reminiscences, Chiefly of the American Revolution in the South.</u> Charleston: Walker & James, 1851; reprinted, Spartanburg, S.C.: The Reprint Co., 1972. CC, CCPL, CLS, SCHS

Biographical sketch of William Henry Drayton (pp. 47-48).

Johnson, Thomas Cary. <u>Scientific Interests in the Old South.</u> New York: D. Appleton-Century Co., 1936. CC, CCPL, CLS

Scientific interests of Maria Henrietta Drayton, her son, Lewis R. Gibbes, and Gov. John Drayton (pp. 124, 128, 134).

Jones, E. Alfred. <u>American Members of the Inns of Court.</u> London: St. Catherine Press, 1924. CLS

Mention of Stephen Fox Drayton, brother of John, Drayton Hall builder; biographical sketch of William Drayton (1733-90) (pp. 64-65); William Henry Drayton mentioned (pp. 149, 220).

Jones, Samuel. <u>The Siege of Charleston, and the Operations on the South Atlantic Coast in the War Among the States.</u> New York: Neale Publishing Co., 1911. CC, CLS, SCHS

Gen. Thomas Drayton at the Battle of Port Royal and later in the war (pp. 56-76). Cmdr. Percival Drayton at Port Royal (p. 55); at James Island, 1862 (p. 101); in attack on Charleston Harbor, 1863 (pp. 168-73).

Kent, William. <u>Designs of Inigo Jones</u>. London: 1727. CC

   The overmantel in the Great Hall of Drayton Hall was copied (with some
   changes) from Plate 64 of this book. Jones was a 17th-century exponent
   of the Palladian architectural style as exemplified at Drayton Hall.

Kimball, Fiske. <u>American Architecture</u>. Indianapolis: Bobbs-Merrill, 1928;
   reprinted, New York: AMS Press, 1970. CC, CLS

   Mention of Drayton Hall portico: "The great portico...which won for
   John Drayton's solid Carolina House the extravagant name of Drayton's
   palace" (p. 48). (See <u>South Carolina Gazette</u> advertisement, Newspapers,
   Part I.)

_____. <u>Domestic Architecture of the American Colonies and
   of the Early Republic</u>. New York: Charles Scribner's Sons, 1922. CC,
   CLS

   Architectural elements at Drayton Hall mentioned (pp. 65, 88, 89, 99, 107).

King, Edward. <u>The Great South: A Record of Journeys in Louisiana, Texas, The
   Indian Territory, Missouri, Arkansas, Mississippi, Alabama, Georgia, Florida,
   South Carolina, North Carolina, Kentucky, Tennessee, Virginia, West Virginia
   and Maryland</u>. Hartford: American Publishing Co., 1875. CC, CCPL, SCHS

   "Along the Ashley, the old manorial houses and estates, like Drayton Hall
   and the Middleton homestead, stand like sorrowful ghosts lamenting the past"
   (p. 451). Post War Between the States rice plantation life on the Combahee
   River, S.C., described (pp. 429-437). Charleston: description, historical
   anecdotes, reconstruction politics (pp. 438-449).

La Rochefoucault-Liancourt, Duke de. <u>Travels through the United States of North
   America, the Country of the Iroquois, and Upper Canada</u>. 2 vols. London: R.
   Phillips, 1799. CLS

   Volume 1: "We stopped to dine with Dr. [Charles] Drayton at Drayton Hall.
   The house is an ancient building, but convenient and good; and the garden
   is better laid out, better cultivated and stocked with good trees, than any
   I have hitherto seen. In order to have a fine garden, you have nothing to
   do but to let the trees remain standing here and there, or in clumps, to
   plant bushes in front of them, and arrange the trees according to their
   height. Dr. Drayton's father, who was also a physician, began to lay out
   the garden on this principle; and his son, who is passionately fond of a
   counrty life, has pursued the same plan" (pp. 591-92).

   Uncorroborated statement: The Hon. John Drayton, father of Dr. Charles
   Drayton I, was not a physician according to all available information.
   Description of Charleston area, climate, slavery, society, education,
   etc. (pp. 554-59, 574-84); rice cultivation and the Elms Plantation (pp.
   586-88); several Ashley River plantations described, including Middleton

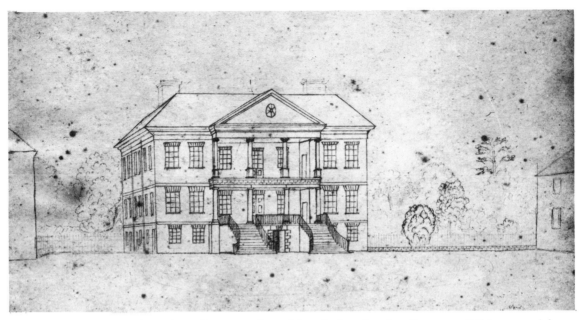

Figure 3: Land facade, from a sketchbook by Lewis Reeves Gibbes, mid-1840s. Gibbes was a great-grandson of John Drayton (ca. 1716-1779) for whom Drayton Hall was built. This sketch provides the only evidence of the appearance of the low wall and fence that joined the dependencies to the house. (Courtesy of the Drayton family--Louis Schwartz photograph)

Figure 4: Land facade, before 1886. This is the only known photographic record of the brick dependencies that flanked the house on the land side. (Photocopy courtesy of Historic Charleston Foundation)

Figure 5: River facade, Lewis Reeves Gibbes Sketchbook, mid-1840s.
(Courtesy of the Drayton family--Louis Schwartz photograph)

Figure 6: River facade, date unknown. (Photocopy courtesy of Historic
Charleston Foundation)

Place (pp. 590-93). (Excerpts quoted in several sources, including Page [see Books, Part I].)

Lashey, Dolores C. Legacy of Beauty. Columbia, S.C.: State Printing Co., 1969. CC, CCPL

The book deals primarily with John Grimke Drayton's creation of the present Magnolia Gardens. Description of Drayton Hall gardens in Charles Drayton's time (apparently from Gov. John Drayton's and David Ramsay's descriptions) (p. 4). Description of gardens at the Drayton plantation, Magnolia (1820s) (pp. 7-8, 15-16).

Lathrop, Elise. Historic Houses of Early America. New York: Tudor Publishing Co., 1936. CCPL, CLS

Customary description and historical anecdotes plus a ghost story: "Another charming old place, Drayton Hall, is in excellent condition, as regards the house, but the grounds are neglected and sadly fallen from former days, since its owner visits it but seldom." "This property and the world-famed Magnolia Gardens were originally one estate; then it was divided between two brothers..." (pp. 50-51). "[Drayton Hall] was suspected of having a ghost, and many were the guests who, given a certain bedroom, retired, only to flee from the room with stories of the ghost they had seen. Later a more intrepid visitor did indeed awaken to see a figure in white, which vanished even as he watched it, but he discovered that the supposed ghost had left a substantial impress on the bed where she [the ghost] had appeared to be sitting. It was discovered the next day that the visitant was not a ghost, but a sleepwalker daughter of the house. The gentleman 'laid' the ghost, and married the daughter."

Errata: "This property and the world-famed Magnolia Gardens were originally one estate." The Drayton Hall property was not in the Drayton family until 1738 when it was acquired by John Drayton who bought Magnolia from his nephew, Judge William Drayton, in 1774. The estate was again divided after John's death in 1779. "Much of the building material was brought from England." The National Trust for Historic Preservation architectural study of the house indicates that probably only the columns, fireplace tiles and marble fireplace fronts were imported. "Lord Cornwallis occupied the house while its owner was attending the Continental Congress in Philadelphia...." William Henry Drayton, who died while attending the Continental Congress in 1779, presumably never owned Drayton Hall. If Lord Cornwallis occupied the house, he did so in 1780 when it was apparently in the possession of Rebecca Perry Drayton, widow of John, Drayton Hall builder. "John Davis...speaks of Drayton Hall as 'a venerable mansion'." This statement applies to the first house at Magnolia, not Drayton Hall. "One of the descendants of the Draytons, a Grimke, was obliged to change his name to Drayton, that he might inherit the property." John Grimke, grandson of John, Drayton Hall builder, took the name of Drayton in order to inherit Magnolia, not Drayton Hall.

Uncorroborated statements: "The real front is toward the river." The land side of the house can also justifiably be called the front because of its portico. "Mrs. Leiding is responsible for the statement that the seal of South Carolina was designed by...Arthur Middleton...[and] Chief Justice Drayton." This statement was not, as Lathrop's wording implies, concocted by Leiding (see Books, Part I), but is found in John Drayton's memoirs (see Books, Part I).

Leiding, Harriette Kershaw. <u>Charleston: Historic and Romantic</u>. Philadelphia: J.B. Lippincott Co., 1931. CC, CCPL, CLS, SCHS

The Drayton family and individual family members mentioned. No mention of Drayton Hall.

_____. <u>Historic Houses of South Carolina</u>. Philadelphia, J.B. Lippincott Co., 1921. CCPL, CLS, SCHS

Description similar to Lathrop's (see Books, Part I) and Woolson's (see Magazines and Journals, Part I). "The letters of Eliza Lucas abound in reference to festal days at Drayton Hall and other mansions on the Ashley, and it is said that it was at Drayton Hall that she first met the man who later became her husband, Chief Justice Pinckney." Paragraph beginning "Drayton Hall was built in 1740" and ending "...the old mansion was never completed" is based on Woolson's article and repeats its errors (pp. 202-4). Quote from La Rochefoucault-Liancourt (1796) (see Books, Part I) (p. 204).

Lesesne, Thomas Petigru. <u>History of Charleston County, South Carolina</u>. Charleston: A.H. Cawston, 1931. CC, CCPL, CLS

Biographical sketch of Charles Henry Drayton, Jr., owner of Drayton Hall (pp. 186-89).

Lincoln, F.S. <u>Charleston: Photographic Studies by F.S. Lincoln</u>. New York: Corinthian Publications, 1946. CC, CCPL, CLS

Not paginated. Four full-page photographs of Drayton Hall, all showing aspects of the land front, including one close-up of the lower portico and one of the side doors of the portico.

Lockwood, Alice G.B., ed. <u>Gardens of Colony and State</u>. New York: Charles Scribner's Sons, 1934. SCHS

Descriptions of the Drayton Hall garden by La Rochefoucault-Liancourt and Ramsay (see both Secondary Sources, Books) quoted (pp. 221-22). The editor is "quite certain" that the avenue approaching Drayton Hall was "formally treated," perhaps with "twin lakes suggesting those at Middleton Place." General description of plantation gardens in the Charleston area and the plants used (p. 220). Other plantation gardens in low country South Carolina (pp. 215-33). John Davis' description of Ocean Plantation, Magnolia and Drayton Hall quoted (pp. 223-28).

I. BOOKS

Mackey, Robert. <u>The letters of Robert Mackey to his Wife</u>. Edited by Walter C.
Hartridge. Athens: University of Georgia Press, 1949. CCPL, CLS

Letters (Dec. 1809-Jan. 1810) from Charleston and elsewhere by a traveling
merchant. Little detail on the places he visited. "Mr. Drayton" (not
identified further) mentioned briefly (pp. 198, 199, 204).

McClure, Harlan, and Hodges, Vernon. <u>South Carolina Architecture 1670-1970</u>.
Columbia: South Carolina Tricentennial Commission, 1970. CC, CCPL,
CLS, SCHS

Descriptive paragraph emphasizing Palladian influence and the architectural importance of the Drayton Hall portico; photograph of the land
front (pp. 10-11).

McCowen, George S., Jr. <u>The British Occupation of Charleston, 1780-82</u>.
Columbia: Univeristy of S.C. Press, 1972. CC, CCPL, CLS

Charles Drayton's efforts to remain neutral during the occupation (pp.
73-74).

Middleton, Alicia Hopton. <u>Life in Carolina and New England during the Nineteenth
Century</u>. Bristol, R.I.: privately printed 1929. CLS, SCHS

Reminiscences, assisted by family papers, of one who remembered antebellum
plantation life on the Ashley River. Middleton Place descriptions (pp.
65-68 and 152-53); description of Magnolia (p. 92). Drayton Hall: ...with-
out special attraction of grounds, the house was the finest on the river and
fortunately, by some caprice, was not burned by the Federal troops, being
the only one spared on the Ashley River" (p. 92).

Erratum: Two houses on the other side of the river survived the War
Between the States, but earthquake and fire claimed both by the early
1900s.

Millar, John Fitzhugh. <u>The Architects of the American Colonies</u>. Barre,
Mass.: Barre Publications, 1968. CC, CLS

"Three names present themselves as being claimants to the title of
architect(s) of a group of eight early buildings. They are John Wood,
who died in 1744; Mr. Johns, who arrived in Charleston in 1698; ...John
Rich, who died in 1745, and who owned five pattern books. Rich sounds
the most likely. In fact, we might...suggest that Rich was the architect and Wood the joiner responsible for the excellent woodwork, especially that at Drayton Hall" (p. 98). Customary description of the house.

Errata: "The...ornamentation is absolutely intact with the exception
of pieces of two mantels that were replaced around 1800. ...the Victor-

ians did not touch it at all." Three mantels were replaced in 1802. Most of the ceilings are replacements; the ceiling in the Great Hall is Victorian (ca. 1860).

Uncorroborated statements: The speculation about the architect is uncorroborated, as Millar points out. His list of architects is apparently based on Ravenel, B. (see Books, Part I); see Cohen (Books, Part I) and Prime (Books, Part II) for other possible architects. "The original front of the house faced the river." Both east and west facades can justifiably be called fronts. "The dependencies, about which we know nothing." There are photographs showing the dependencies (sometime before 1886) as plain two-story brick structures. National Trust for Historic Preservation archaeological excavation of the southeast flanker revealed additional information. "Many heavy and rich overmantels from William Kent's book ...." Other sources cite only one overmantel, that of the Great Hall, as copied from Kent's book. Other buildings that Millar attributes to the same architect(s): Brick House, Edisto Island, 1725; Archdale Hall, Ashley River, 1706; Charles Pinckney House, Charleston, 1745-46; Fenwick Hall, John's Island, circa 1730; Crowfield, Goose Creek, 1730; unidentified Ashley River plantation [from Fraser, Books, Part I]; Thomas Rose House, Charleston, 1735. Pictures and descriptions of these buildings (pp. 99-102).

Molloy, Robert. _Charleston: A Gracious Heritage_. New York: D. Appleton-Century Co., 1947. CCPL, CLS, SCHS

Drayton Hall mentioned. Repeats story that it was Cornwallis's headquarters (pp. 60, 72), from Woolson (see Magazines and Journals, Part I). Description and story that the house was saved in 1865 because of use as a smallpox hospital (p. 193).

Errata: "...when Negro troops, during the Civil War, burned and destroyed a number of plantations, they left Drayton Hall strictly alone, when its owner at that time, a physician, had the presence of mind to turn it into a pesthouse." Negro troops were not solely responsible for the destruction, and Dr. John Drayton evidently was not the owner, but was taking care of the house for his nephew, Charles H. Drayton IV.

Morrison, Andrew. _The City of Charleston and State of South Carolina_. Richmond: Andrews & Baptist, [ca. 1889]. CC, SCHS

Guidebook to tourist attractions and commercial establishments. Drayton Hall mentioned, not in detail (pp. 37-38). Drayton phosphate mine mentioned among the smaller companies (p. 111).

Morrison, Hugh. _Early American Architecture: From the First Colonial Settlements to the National Period_. New York: Oxford University Press, 1952. CC, CCPL, CLS

Figure 7: Plate 64, William Kent, The
Designs of Inigo Jones, Vol. 1. (London,
1770 edition). (Courtesy Nathaniel P.
Neblett--Gale S. Alder photograph, NTHP)

Figure 8: Chimneypiece, first floor
great hall, ca. 1937. The design of
the overmantel is derived from Plate
64 of William Kent's Design of Inigo
Jones (London, 1727). (Frances Benjamin Johnston photograph, Library
of Congress)

"The early date seems remarkable, for Drayton Hall is far in advance, architecturally, of contemporary great houses in Virginia. The west or 'land' facade is dominated by a projecting two-story portico...This feature, which stemmed directly from Palladio, was apparently not employed elsewhere in the colonies until the 1750s" (pp. 401-4). "The grandeur of the plan, with its monumental effects and excellent circulation between rooms and porches, and the advanced character of the architectural details point to something more than an amateur designer using architectural books; they suggest a professional architect, perhaps one of English training. But as to who he may have been there is no hint" (p. 404). Photographs of land front and stair hall, elevation of river front, plan of main floor.

Errata: "Two [mantels] were replaced in 1800." Three mantels were replaced in 1802, according to National Trust for Historic Preservation architectural research. "The entrance door and window frames are all of wood." The portico pillars are Portland stone.

Moultrie, Alexander. _An Appeal to the People, on the Conduct of a Certain Public Body in South Carolina, Respecting Col. Drayton and Col. Moultrie._ Charleston: Markland, M'Iver & Co., 1794. CLS

Defense of activities on behalf of the French revolutionaries by Stephen Drayton, nephew of John, Drayton Hall builder, and son of Thomas Drayton.

Moultrie, William. _Memoirs of the American Revolution._ 2 vols. New York: printed for the author, 1802; reprinted, New York: Arno Press, 1968. CC, CCPL, CLS, SCHS

Volume 1 contains several mentions of William Henry Drayton's activities on behalf of the Revolution. More detail on these activities in Drayton, J., and Dabney (both, Books, Part I).

Mowat, Charles L. _East Florida as a British Province 1763-1784._ University of California Press, 1943. CLS

Traces the career of William Drayton as chief justice of East Florida, 1765-78 (pp. 44-49, 70, 84-105).

National Trust for Historic Preservation. _Annual Report 1974-1975._ Washington, D.C.: Preservation Press. 1975. SCHS

Acquisition of Drayton Hall by the Trust; explanation of the cooperative plan with South Carolina Department of Parks, Recreation & Tourism and Historic Charleston Foundation (pp. 21, 23).

Page, Marian. _Historic Houses Restored and Preserved._ New York: Whitney Library of Design, 1976. CCPL, CLS

Good treatment of the architecture and social background of the house, with quotations from a number of 18th and 19th-century descriptions of the house (pp. 33-41). Quotations from the National Trust for Historic Preservation architectural report provide the best published explanation of the National Trust's preservation philosophy regarding Drayton Hall.

Errata: The description of John Drayton, the builder (pp. 39-40) is based on the prejudiced views of his grandson, Gov. John Drayton, and is probably not entirely fair. "1712 – John Drayton is born." He was born between June 1714 and June 1716. "December 1825 issue of Harper's ...." Actually 1875. "John Davis...moved to Drayton Hall in May." Thomas Drayton, Davis's employer, lived at Magnolia, not Drayton Hall. "The entrance door and three windows above it are framed by...carved Portland stone...." The door and window frames are of wood. Only the portico pillars are Portland stone.

Palladio, Andrea. The Four Books of Architecture. (four books in one volume)
    London: Isaac Ware, 1738; reprinted, New York: Dover Publications,
    1965. CC, CLS

Book II contains numerous illustrations of the type of plans that must have influenced Drayton Hall's design.

Phillips, Ulrich Bonnell. Life and Labor in the Old South. Boston: Little,
    Brown, and Co., 1930. CC, CCPL, CLS, SCHS

An overview of many facets of the plantation system and the lives of those involved in it. Low country crops and trade; Charleston buildings and society; education and family life of 18th-century South Carolina planters, quoting J. Davis's description (see Books, Part I) of the Thomas Drayton family; slavery, overseers.

Pinckney, Eliza Lucas. The Letterbook of Eliza Lucas Pinckney, 1739-1762.
    Edited by Elise Pinckney. Chapel Hill: University of North Carolina
    Press, 1972. CC, CCPL, CLS, SCHS

Letters from a plantation near Charleston by the woman responsible for the development of indigo as an important crop. Letter to Mary Drayton (wife of Thomas, the Hon. John Drayton's brother), 1758 (pp. 93-94). Birth of Thomas Drayton, Jr., mentioned, 1759 (p. 137). Death of Thomas Drayton, Sr., and reference to his garden, 1760 (p. 162). Letter to William Henry Drayton, 1761; indications of poor relations between him and his father, John (pp. 169-70).

Powell, Lyman P., ed. Historic Towns of the Southern States. New York:
    G.P. Putnam's Sons, 1900. CC, CLS, SCHS

Chapter on Charleston by Yates Snowden (pp. 249-92) does not mention Drayton Hall and only William Henry of the family, but quotes several in-

teresting travelers' descriptions of Charleston society in the late 18th
and early 19th century.

Proceedings of the State Rights Celebration at Charleston, July 1st, 1830:
    Containing the Speeches of the Hon. Wm. Drayton & Hon. R.Y. Hayne, Who
    were Invited Guests; Also of Langdon Cheves, James Hamilton Jr. and
    Robert J. Turnbull Esqrs. and the Remarks of His Honor, the Intendant,
    H.L. Pinckney, to which is added the Volunteer Toasts Given on the Oc-
    casion. Charleston: A.E. Miller, 1830. CCPL, CLS

Drayton's speech opposed nullification and stated that secession would
be worse than the tariff against which nullification was directed.

Ramsay, David. Ramsay's History of South Carolina. 2 vols. Newberry, S.C.:
    W.J. Duffie, 1858 (1st published 1809); reprinted, Spartanburg, S.C.:
    The Reprint Co., 1959. CC, CCPL, CLS, SCHS

Volume 2 contains a biographical sketch of William Henry Drayton (p.
129) and description of Drayton Hall garden: "It is arranged with ex-
quisite taste and contains an extensive collection of trees, shrubs and
flowers which are natives of the country. Among many other valuable
exotics, great number of viburnum tinus [Laurestinus - a large flowering
shrub of the honeysuckle family], and of gardenias, which are perfectly
naturalized to the soil, grow there with enchanting luxuriance; but the
principal object of the proprietor [Charles Drayton I] has been to make
an elegant and concentrated display of the native botanic riches of
Carolina, in which he has succeeded to the delight and admiration of all
visitants" (ibid). Maria Drayton (daughter of Charles) mentioned as a
"distinguished" botanist (p. 195). Volume 2 also contains general information on the way of life, virtues and vices of South Carolinians in
the late 18th and early 19th centuries.

Ravenel, Beatrice St. Julien. Architects of Charleston. 2nd ed. Charleston:
    Carolina Art Association, 1964. CC, CCPL, CLS

No mention of Drayton Hall. Survey of Charleston architects and master
builders before the Revolution (pp. 13-53). William Drayton as an amateur
architect, 1788 (pp. 71-75).

Ravenel, Harriott Horry Rutledge (Mrs. St. Julien Ravenel). Charleston: The
    Place and the People. New York: The Macmillan Co., 1906. CC, CCPL,
    CLS, SCHS

Mention and drawing of Drayton Hall (p. 88); Cornwallis at Drayton Hall
(p. 277); La Rochefoucault-Liancourt's (see Books, Part I) high
opinion of Drayton Hall (p. 382); William Henry, Col. William, Thomas
(the immigrant) and Maria [Henrietta] Drayton mentioned several times.

Errata: Several errors repeated from Woolson article (see Magazines and
Journals, Part I) or repeated from Lathrop (see Books, Part I).

I. BOOKS

_____. _Eliza Pinckney_. New York: Charles Scribner's Sons, 1896; reprinted, Spartanburg, S.C.: The Reprint Co., 1967. CC, CCPL, CLS, SCHS

Biography of a female planter in 18th-century South Carolina. Conjectural description of a "festal day" at Drayton Hall; dress, food, drink, etc.; mention of the "wide lawn stretching to the bank," and the fact that the house (in 1896) "has been restored to something of its former state" (pp. 42-49); "...the Masters Drayton" at school in England, 1759 (p. 181); Thomas Drayton's marriage (p. 188); description of Pinckney house in Charleston, similar in some respects to Drayton Hall (pp. 110-112).

Ravenel, Henry William. _The Private Journal of Henry William Ravenel, 1859-1881_. Edited by Arney Robinson Childs. Columbia: University of South Carolina Press, 1947. CC, CCPL, CLS, SCHS

Life near Aiken, S.C., in the era of the War Between the States and Reconstruction. Brief mentions of the Rev. John Grimke Drayton, of Magnolia (offered rectorship of St. Thaddeus Church, Aiken, 1869, but declined) (pp. 339-40). October 24, 1876: "Mrs. Drayton & her children dined with us today. She came in to see Drayton who was arrested yesterday on charge of intimidation of voters" (p. 382). This Drayton has not been identified.

Reynolds, Clifford P., et al., eds. _Biographical Directory of the American Congress, 1774-1961_. Washington: Government Printing Office, 1961. CLS

Brief biographical sketches of Col. William Drayton and William Henry Drayton (pp. 829-30). Better biographical sketches of these and other Draytons are found in the _Dictionary of American Biography_ (see Books, Part I).

Rhett, Robert Goodwyn. _Charleston: An Epic of Carolina_. Richmond: Garrett & Massie, 1940. CCPL, CLS

Mention of John Drayton and Drayton Hall (p. 103), William Henry Drayton (pp. 103-116, 126, 145), Col. William Drayton (p. 197).

Rice, James Henry, Jr. _The Aftermath of Glory_. Charleston: Walker, Evans & Cogswell Co., 1934. CC, CCPL, CLS

No mention of Drayton Hall. The Draytons of Magnolia Plantation (pp. 217-19); William Henry Drayton (p. 231).

Rippy, J. Fred. _Joel R. Poinsett, Versatile American_. Durham, N.C.: Duke University Press, 1935. CC, CCPL, CLS

William Drayton's activities to preserve the Union, 1830-33, mentioned several times.

Rogers, George C., Jr. Charleston in the Age of the Pinckneys. Norman, Okla.: University of Oklahoma Press, 1969. CC, CCPL, CLS, SCHS

An overview of Charleston's history and culture up to the War Between the States. Drayton Hall mentioned briefly (pp. 46, 66, 86); 1762 advertisement for a horse at stud at Drayton Hall (pp. 112-13); 1749 description of the fair at Ashley Ferry (near Drayton Hall) (p. 13). Several mentions of Judge William Drayton, William Henry Drayton, Col. William Drayton.

Erratum: "The British...marched...to Ashley Ferry Town near Drayton Hall, whence they crossed to Gibb's [sic] Landing..." (p. 46). Apparently one group crossed at Drayton Hall, two at Magnolia and the baggage and its guards at Ashley Ferry. (See Uhlendorf, Books, Part I.)

Salley, A[lexander]. S., Jr., ed. Warrants for Lands in South Carolina, 1672-1711. 2nd ed. revised by R. Nicholas Olsberg. Columbia: University of South Carolina Press, 1973. CC, CLS, SCHS

About a dozen mentions of tracts of lands granted to Thomas Drayton I and/or Thomas Drayton II on New Town Creek (James Island) and several other locations between 1678 and 1709.

Sarles, Frank B., Jr., and Shedd, Charles E. Colonials and Patriots: Historic Places Commemorating Our Forebears, 1700-1783. Volume 6, National Survey of Historic Sites and Buildings, Washington: Government Printing Office, 1964. CC, CCPL, CLS

Summary of the architectural importance of the house (taken largely from Morrison, H. (see Books, Part I; description of the present (1964) condition of house and grounds (pp. 161-62).

Sellers, Leila. Charleston Business on the Eve of the American Revolution. Chapel Hill: University of North Carolina Press, 1934; reprinted, New York: Library Editions, 1970. CC, CCPL, CLS

John Drayton's business transaction with Henry Laurens, 1767 (p. 76). Several mentions of William Henry Drayton and business politics. The book deals with the grade system in which planters and merchants were involved, and the effect of the approaching Revolution on business.

Shaffer, E[dward] T.H. Carolina Gardens. New York: Huntington Press, 1937; Reprinted, New York: Devin-Adair Co., 1963. CC, CCPL, CLS, SCHS

Drayton Hall garden is called one of "the 18 outstanding colonial gardens" in South Carolina (pp. 28, 31). "When peace once more returned [in 1865] but three of the Ashley River houses remained, among them being the stately Drayton Hall which is still occupied and whose garden is tended by a Drayton" (p. 62).

Figure 9: Land facade, stereopticon photograph, ca. 1870. Close inspection of this view, the earliest known photograph of Drayton Hall, reveals that the tympanum was brick and the roof covering was not the metal that appears in all later photographs, nor does the present balustrade appear. (Photocopy courtesy Anna Wells Rutledge and Ernest A. Connally)

Uncorroborated statement: "The present gardens were laid out by an English gardener long before the Revolution." The original gardens were laid out before the Revolution; however, there was probably no trace of the original gardens in the "present gardens" of 1937. Description of the garden by La Rochefoucault-Liancourt quoted (see Books, Part I). John Grimke Drayton's garden at Magnolia described (pp. 65-68).

Simms, William Gilmore [A Southron]. South Carolina in the Revolutionary War. Charleston: Walker & James, 1853. CLS

Quote from John L. Gervais's journal, 29 March 1780, stating that the British crossed the Ashley "at Drayton Hall" (p. 102).

Simons, Albert, and Lapham, Samuel Jr. The Early Architecture of Charleston. Second ed. (First published 1927 under the title, Charleston, South Carolina.) Columbia: University of South Carolina Press, 1970. CC, CCPL, CLS

A study of architecture in the city of Charleston, including the William Drayton House on Gibbes Street (pp. 138-40). No mention of Drayton Hall.

Sirmans, M. Eugene. Colonial South Carolina: A Political History, 1663-1763. Chapel Hill: University of North Carolina Press, 1966. CC, CCPL, SCHS

A good study of the history of the colony, including some social and economic information as well as political. Dominance in the colony of the St. Andrew's Parish "bloc" consisting of the Draytons, Middletons and Bulls mentioned several times.

Smith D.E. Huger. A Charlestonian's Recollection, 1846-1913. Charleston: Carolina Art Association, 1950. CCPL, CLS, SCHS

"We paid two other visits on the road, one of which was at Magnolia, the Drayton place on the Ashley" (p. 94). Rice plantation life at Smithfield on the Combahee in the 1850s (pp. 13-58). Charleston life in the 1850s (pp. 58-67).

Smythe, Augustine T., et al. The Carolina Low-Country. New York: The MacMillan Co., 1931. CC, CCPL, SCHS

Chapters on various subjects: history, folklore, spirituals, etc. Drayton Hall mentioned. Story that the house was saved in 1865 by use as a smallpox hospital (pp. 13, 74-75). Drawing of Drayton Hall land front (facing p. 58). "Before [the Union troops] came [Dr. John] Drayton had taken out the family silverware. As the box containing it was heavy, he was aided by some Negroes in burying it. A smaller box containing an elegant gold service, an English gift to an early bride in the Drayton family, was buried by John Drayton without aid. After the Confederate War he returned to Drayton Hall and found the silverware gone. The gold service, however, was still where he had buried it and is now in Charleston" (pp. 74-75). Note: See Eggleston, Magazines and Journals, Part I, for an illustration of the gold service.

Uncorroborated statements: The story of the burial of the gold and silver services has not been found elsewhere. "John Drayton, a surgeon in the Confederate Army." No other evidence that Dr. Drayton was an army surgeon has been found.

Smythe, Mrs. A.T., et al. <u>South Carolina Women in the Confederacy</u>. 2 vols. Columbia, S.C.: The State Co., 1903. CLS

Numerous mentions of Miss Hester D. Drayton's leadership of the Ladies' Clothing Association in Charleston, which made clothes for Confederate troops throughout the war (vol. 1).

Snowden, Yates, ed. <u>History of South Carolina</u>. 5 vols. Chicago: Lewis Publishing Co., 1920. CCPL, CLS, SCHS

Many references to William Henry Drayton, several to Gov. John Drayton (vol. 1). "General [Thomas F.] and Captain [Percival] Drayton, under two flags, were half-brothers" (vol. 2).

Erratum: Other sources call Thomas F. and Percival Drayton brothers, not half brothers. Taylor (see Magazines and Journals, Part I) lists them both as sons of Col. William Drayton and Ann Gadsden.

Sprunt, Alexander, Jr. <u>Carolina Low-Country Impressions</u>. New York: Devin-Adair Co., 1964. CCPL, CLS

Drayton Hall, drawing and brief text (pp. 122-23). John Grimke Drayton and Magnolia Gardens (pp. 119-20). Little detail on the Draytons or Drayton Hall.

Stevens, William Oliver. <u>Charleston: Historic City of Gardens</u>. New York: Dodd, Mead & Co., 1946. CLS SCHS

Description of the house, based largely on Woolson and Bunce (see Magazines and Journals, Part I).

Errata: "Unfortunately, in devotion to the cause, the owner during the 1860s ripped off the lead on the roof to be used for making Confederate bullets." If there is truth in this story, it refers to lead flashing and guttering on a slate or wood shingle roof. The National Trust for Historic Preservation architectural study indicates that the metal roof postdates 1870. "In 1865 Sherman's army swept over the land....One after another of these great river mansions was burned down." Sherman's army did not come near Charleston; the troops who plundered along the Ashley were from the Union-occupied islands south of Charleston. "While all this was happening, there was a Rear Admiral Percival Drayton with the Union fleet lying off the bar of Charleston harbor." Percival Drayton

never rose higher in rank than captain, and there is no clear evidence
that he was near Charleston when the plantations were plundered.

Uncorroborated statements: The story of the Middleton punch bowl lost
in the Ashley on the way to a wedding at Drayton Hall is traditional, but
has not been confirmed by documents (pp. 197-98).

Stoney, Samuel Gaillard. Plantations of the Carolina Low Country. Charleston:
Carolina Art Association, 1939. CC, CLS

Description of the house, story of its rescue in 1865 (pp. 58-59); several mentions of the house on other pages (check index); excellent illustrations (interior and exterior photographs, plans, elevations of exterior and of several rooms) (pp. 142-61).

Trenholm, Alicia Middleton. Flat Rock, North Carolina: A Sketch of the Past.
Asheville, N.C.: The Inland Press, 1908. CLS, SCHS

A brief description of the summer resort that the Draytons and many other
Charleston-area families frequented from the early 19th century on. Mention of Draytons (p. 9), John Grimke Drayton (p. 25).

Turnbull, Robert J. Bibliography of South Carolina, 1563-1950. 6 vols.
Charlottesville: University Press of Virginia, 1956-1960. CC, CLS, SCHS

See the index for works by Drayton family members not available to this
bibliographer.

Tuomey, Michael. Report on the Geology of South Carolina. Columbia, S.C.:
A.S. Johnston, 1848. CLS, CCPL

Mention of marl stone "gathered from the lawn" at Drayton Hall (p. 164).
(Mining this stone for the phosphate it contains became important for the
Draytons after the War Between the States.)

Uhlendorf, Bernhard A., ed. and trans. The Siege of Charleston with an
Account of the Province of South Carolina: Diaries and Letters of Hessian
Officers from the von Jungkenn Papers in the William L. Clements Library.
Ann Arbor: University of Michigan Press, 1930; reprinted, New York:
Arno Press, 1968. SCHS, CC, CLS

Gen. Leslie's division of the British army camped "at Drayton's" (presumably Drayton Hall, 23-29 March 1780) (p. 219); 29 March, "The boats
under the command of Captain Tonken, with an escort of two armed boats,
came tonight as far as Major General Leslie's quarters [at "Drayton's"],
and at break of day the jägers, the light infantry, and the 1st Battalion
of British Grenadiers embarked and landed at Tom Fuller's [Ashley Bluff
Plantation, above Drayton Hall]....The second contingent...later crossed
at Tom Drayton's house [Magnolia]" (pp. 223-25).

I. BOOKS

Wallace, David Duncan. *The Life of Henry Laurens*. New York: G.P. Putnam's
Sons, 1915. CC, CCPL, CLS, SCHS

Biography of a merchant and politician in Revolutionary-period Charles
Town. John Drayton mentioned (p. 51); William Henry Drayton mentioned
frequently (pp. 152-346).

Walsh, Richard. *Charleston's Sons of Liberty: A Study of the Artisans,
1763-1769*. Columbia: University of South Carolina Press, 1959. CC, CCPL,
CLS, SCHS

Three brief mentions of William Henry Drayton. One chapter surveys the
trades and small businesses of Charles Town in the late colonial period.
The remainder of the book details the political involvement of artisans
in the Revolutionary period.

Waterman, Thomas Tileston. *The Dwellings of Colonial America*. Chapel Hill:
University of North Carolina Press, 1950. CLS

Typical description of Drayton Hall and three photographs (pp. 2, 72,
73, 77).

Whitelaw, Robert N.S., and Levkoff, Alice F. *Charleston Come Hell or High
Water*. Columbia, S.C.: R.L. Bryan Co., 1975. CC, CCPL, SCHS

A collection of old photographs. Important photo of Drayton Hall showing the flankers before the north one was destroyed in the 1886 earthquake (p. 59). An oak at Drayton Hall, early 1900s (p. 170). Land front
of Drayton Hall, 1930s (p. 224).

Year Book, City of Charleston, 1886. "Interesting Private Letters, Written by
Carolinians in the Last Century." Charleston: Walker, Evans & Cogswell.
CC, CCPL, CLS, SCHS

Letter from William Henry Drayton to Col. John Laurens, 1778, congratu-
lating Laurens on "the glory...gained in the late action on Rhode Island,"
but warning him not to risk his life unnecessairly (pp. 338-39). (Laurens
was killed in 1782 in one of the last skirmishes of the Revolutionary War.)

MAGAZINES AND JOURNALS

Barnwell, Joseph W., ed. "Correspondence of Hon. Arthur Middleton."
South Carolina Historical and Genealogical Magazine 27 (1926):
1-29, 51-80, 107-55. CC, CCPL, CLS, SCHS

Criticism (from Edward Rutledge and Charles C. Pinckney) of Dr. Charles
Drayton's efforts to remain neutral during the British occupation (1782)
(pp. 8, 12, 61). Thomas Drayton, Jr., (of Magnolia) has joined Francis

Figure 10: Ceiling, first floor drawing room, Lewis Reeves Gibbes Sketchbook, mid-1840s. This rendering shows
the complete design before a portion of
the plaster fell. (Courtesy of the
Drayton family--Louis Schwartz photograph)

Figure 11: Ceiling, first floor
drawing room, 1973. The only major
decorative plaster ceiling dating
from the period of construction of
the house. (Louis Schwartz photograph)

Marion's troops "to the surprise of everybody" (p. 61). Letters to
William Henry Drayton concerning his political activities, 1775-76
(pp. 117-26). Letter from Dr. Charles Drayton to William Henry Drayton,
1775, dealing with British activity in Charleston Harbor and patriot
countermeasures (pp. 136-37).

Brown, Ralph H. "Governor Drayton's Contribution to Geography." South
 Carolina Historical and Genealogical Magazine 39 (April 1938): 68-72.
 CC, CCPL, CLS, SCHS

Discusses Drayton's View of South Carolina (see Books, Part I) as "a
regional description of unusual quality" and the possible influences on
Drayton's work as well as contemporary opinions of the book.

_____. "Materials Bearing Upon the Geography of the Atlantic
 Seaboard, 1790 to 1810." Annals of the Association of American Geographers
 28 (1938): 201-31. CLS

Gov. John Drayton's View of South Carolina discussed (pp. 218-20). See
preceding entry by the same author for a fuller treatment.

Bunce, Oliver Bell. "Charleston and its Suburbs." Appleton's Journal of
 Literature, Science and Art, 15 July 1871, pp. 57-61. Reprinted in
 William Cullen Bryant, ed. Picturesque America, or The Land We Live
 In. 2 vols. New York: D. Appleton & Co., 1872. (Vol. 1, pp. 198-211).
 CC, SCHS

Drayton Hall description: "Of all the planters' houses that stood along
the Ashley, but one remains, and this is abandoned. 'Drayton Hall' is
a large brick mansion, standing in the centre of grounds of a park-like
character. The rooms are wainscoted from floor to ceiling, the fireplaces are lined with old-fashioned colored tiles, and the mantels are
richly carved, but the building was never entirely finished" (p. 60,
Appleton's Journal). Description of gardens at Magnolia (ibid.).

Errata: "The wainscot, the tiles, the carved mantels, and marble columns,
were all imported" (p. 60). The National Trust for Historic Preservation
architectural study indicates that the columns and tiles probably were
imported, but the wainscot and mantels probably were not. "The building
was never entirely finished." The story that the house is incomplete
seems to be an exaggerated version of a statement in the 1860 newspaper
article, "St. Andrew's Parish" (see Newspapers, Part I).

Uncorroborated statements: Drayton Hall is not known to be an "exact copy
of an English mansion" (p. 60); John Drayton, the builder, is not known to
have been betrothed to any lady who died when the house was under construction.

Clinton, Sir Henry. "Sir Henry Clinton's 'Journal of the Siege of Charleston,
    1780'." Edited by William T. Bulger. <u>South Carolina Historical Magazine</u>
    66 (July 1965): 147-74. CC, CCPL, CLS, SCHS

    "Marched to Draytons. Reconnoitered landing; chose the lower; over-per-
    suaded by [Maj. Gen.] Rob[ertson]. Landed at upper without a shot;
    halted that night at Ashley Ferry" (p. 149). Editor identifies "Draytons,"
    site of British crossing of Ashley River, 29 March 1780, as Drayton Hall
    (p. 147).

Cornforth, John. "The Future of Drayton Hall." <u>Country Life</u>, 1 August 1974.
    SCHS

    An English perspective on the story of Drayton Hall, its architectural
    uniqueness, possible architectural influences, brief history of the
    estate, efforts of the National Trust for Historic Preservation and
    Historic Charleston Foundation to save it. British and American preser-
    vation compared. The article repeats Gov. John Drayton's critical view
    of John, Drayton Hall builder. Seven photographs of exterior and interior,
    plus an early anonymous design of what is apparently Drayton Hall, with
    elaborate flankers.

    Erratum: "It is many years since rice or indigo were the crops at Drayton."
    Rice was never grown at Drayton Hall, and there is no evidence of indigo
    being grown there.

Eggleston, Edward. "The Colonists at Home." <u>Century Magazine</u>, April 1885,
    pp. 873-92. CCPL, CLS

    The article discusses homes, furnishings, food, drink and clothing through-
    out the colonies. Brief description of Drayton Hall (p. 875); engravings
    of Drayton family heirlooms (watch and gold tea service) (pp. 879-80).

Elfe, Thomas. "The Thomas Elfe Account Book 1768-1775." <u>South Carolina
    Historical and Genealogical Magazine</u> 35 (January 1934); 42 (January 1941).
    CC, CCPL, CLS, SCHS

    Elfe was a significant cabinetmaker who made or mended many pieces of
    furniture (including a child's coffin) for John Drayton of Drayton Hall.
    Elfe gives prices and brief descriptions of items. For example: "John
    Drayton; 6th [Jan. 1772] For a Breakfast Table ₤ 16." "John Drayton;
    [Feb. 1772] For Mending 6 mahogany Chairs [₤] 2.10." Other mentions of
    John Drayton in index.

Gee, Wilson. "South Carolina Botanists: Biography and Bibliography." <u>Bul-
    letin of the University of South Carolina</u>, 72 (September 1918). CLS, SCHS

    Biographical sketch of Gov. John Drayton (pp. 24-28), focusing on his
    <u>Carolinian Florist</u> and <u>View of South Carolina</u> (see Books, Part I).

I. MAGAZINES AND JOURNALS

Grayson, William John. "The Confederate Diary of William John Grayson."
Edited by Elmer L. Puryear. South Carolina Historical Magazine 63
(July and October 1962): 137-49, 214-26. CC, CCPL, CLS, SCHS

Gen. Thomas F. Drayton mentioned (p. 147). Commentary on the War Between
the States by a former Union advocate in low country South Carolina; very
dissatisfied with the Confederate government and its conduct of the war.

Hayne, Isaac. "Records Kept by Colonel Isaac Hayne." South Carolina
Historical and Genealogical Magazine 10 (July 1909); 12 (January 1911).
CC, CCPL, CLS, SCHS

Consists mainly of birth, death and marriage records, circa 1743-79.
Draytons noted in July, October 1909, January, April 1910 issues. Birth
and death records of Hayne's slaves and some plantation records dealing
with white employees and issue of supplies to slaves (January 1911).

Izard, George. "Diary of a Journey by George Izard, 1815-1816." Edited by
Harold W. Ryan. South Carolina Historical Magazine 53 (April 1952):
67-76. CC, CCPL, CLS, SCHS

The author dines with Dr. Charles Drayton and his neighbor, Ralph Stead
Izard, at Drayton Hall, 31 January 1816 (p. 76), no details.

"Journal of the Council of Safety." Collections of the South-Carolina
Historical Society 2 (1858): 22-74. Article continued in 3 (1859);
35-271. CLS, SCHS

Many references to William Henry Drayton's activities in the early years
of the American Revolution. (He was a member of the Council of Safety.)

Leland, Harriott Cheves, and Greene, Harlan, eds. " 'Robbing the Owner or
Saving the Property from Destruction?' Paintings in the Middleton Place
House." South Carolina Historical Magazine 78 (April 1977):
92-103. CC, CCPL, CLS, SCHS

The article deals mainly with the plundering of Middleton Place farther
up the Ashley.

Description of Drayton Hall by Dr. Henry O. Marcy of the Union Army,
February 1865: "The great driveway leading to the house was through a
double row of Live Oaks of two Centuries growth.... These Oaks are said
to be the finest grove in the South. The many acres of gardens devoted
to Azaleas in variety and beauty equal ... the Middleton gardens" (p. 95).

"The Manor house at the Drayton plantation was not burned. It was built
of bricks, of two stories with a hip roof and would have been considered
very elegant if not compared with the finer Middleton House" (p. 95).

Note: This is the only contemporary description that considers the Middleton house "finer" than Drayton Hall. See La Rochefoucault-Liancourt (Books, Part I) for the opposite opinion.

Erratum: "...for three generations..." Drayton Hall was owned by the 5th generation since John, Drayton Hall builder.

Uncorroborated statement: "Live Oaks of two Centuries growth." It is unlikely that the avenue is older than the house which was about 125 years old in 1865, although some of the individual trees on the grounds are undoubtedly older.

Leland, Isabella Middleton, ed. "Middleton Correspondence, 1861-1865." South Carolina Historical Magazine 63 (January 1962); 65 (April 1964). CC, CCPL, CLS, SCHS

The war and the home front as seen by an Ashley River planter family. "One of Mr. Tom Drayton's [probably Gen. Thomas F. Drayton] negroes was taken by the Yankees on board of a ship. The officers asked him if he knew who Mr. Percy Drayton [Capt. Percival Drayton, U.S.N., brother of Thomas F.] was, and what the Southerners thought of him - 'they couldn't think worse of anybody than they do of him. Sir, the fact is, we all spises him, Sir. Indeed, tha's just what we do,' was the answer...." (Vol. 63, p. 63, April 25, 1862).

Manigault, Peter. "The Letterbook of Peter Manigault." Edited by Maurice A. Crouse. South Carolina Historical Magazine 70 (April and July 1969): 79-96, 177-195. CC, CCPL, CLS, SCHS

Purchase of ₤1000 (sterling) worth of land at Wappoo Creek in 1770 by John Drayton, Jr. (Either a son of Thomas, brother of John, Drayton Hall builder, or--less probably--John himself, who was called John Drayton, Jr., on a parish record in 1737.) (See Webber, Magazines and Journals, Part I). Also mention of his secure financial position (July, p. 185).

McCormack, Helen G. "Expatriate Portraits: Charlestonians in Museums Outside Charleston." Antiques, November 1970, pp. 787-93. CC, CCPL, CLS

Portrait of Col. William Drayton, 1818, by Samuel F.B. Morse reproduced (pp. 792-93); now in the White House.

Nichols, Frederick D. "Drayton Hall, Plantation House of the Drayton Family." Antiques, April 1970, pp. 576-78. CC, CCPL, CLS

"Drayton Hall is unquestionably one of the finest of all Georgian Mansions in North America...it shows what the splendor of the Carolina Low Country was like." Quote from La Rochefoucault-Liancourt (see Books, Part I). Discusses architectural influences from Palladio, Kent's Designs of Inigo Jones (see Books, Part I) and Colin Campbell. "The interiors survive

architecturally in almost their original condition, and this fact, plus
their superb quality, makes them one of the great treasures of eighteenth-
century American art." Photographs of land front, fireplace in Great Hall,
wall and fireplace in first floor drawing room, settee from Drayton Hall
now in Heyward-Washington House. Engravings of Kent's Plate 64 (source for
Great Hall overmantel) and of one of Colin Campbell's designs with some
similarities to Drayton Hall.

Pinckney, Thomas, Jr. "Letters from Thomas Pinckney Jr. to Harriott Pinckney."
    South Carolina Historical and Genealogical Magazine 41 (July 1940):
    99-116. CC, CCPL, CLS, SCHS

    Letter of 22 December 1801: Mention of Dr. Charles Drayton; gossip about
    the upcoming wedding of Paul Trapier and Sarah Shubrick by "the Universal
    Chronicle, Miss Hannah Drayton" (daughter of Judge Wm. Drayton, grand-
    niece of John, Drayton Hall builder) (p. 102).

Rogers, George C., Jr. "The History of Charleston, 1670-1860." Antiques,
    April 1970, pp. 540-41. CC, CCPL, CLS

    A brief summary of the period with mention of Col. William Drayton. For
    more, see Rogers (Books, Part I).

Salley, A.S., Jr., ed. "Abstracts from the Records of the Court of Ordinary
    of the Province of South Carolina, 1692-1700." South Carolina Historical
    and Genealogical Magazine 10 (July, October 1909): 136-44, 236-44.
    CC, CCPL, CLS, SCHS

    Thomas Drayton directed to appraise an estate, 1698 (July, p. 138).
    Thomas Drayton purchases 100 acres of public land, 1697 (October, p. 238).

Satterthwaite, Ann. "A New Meaning for Landscape." Historic Preservation 25
    (July-September 1973): 4-9. CC, CLS

    Drayton Hall is used as an example of the current emphasis on preserving
    the surrounding environment as well as historic buildings. Nine photo-
    graphs of the house (interior and exterior) and grounds, two of which
    were taken circa 1910.

    Uncorroborated statement: "...the grounds at Drayton Hall were never
    formally landscaped." Gov. John Drayton and others have mentioned the
    use of an English gardener, who may have created a garden that was formal
    by today's standards if not by those of the 18th century.

Shaffer, E[dward] J.H. "The Ashley River and its Gardens." National Geo-
    graphic, May 1926, pp. 524-50. CC, CCPL, CLS

    The author apparently did not see the house, and based his description
    on published sources. The Duke de la Rochefoucault-Liancourt's 1796
    description of Drayton Hall and Middleton Place are quoted extensively,

but Shaffer's other information on the house is not always reliable. His information on Magnolia Gardens and Middleton Place seems to be more accurate (pp. 524 and 531).

Simms, William Gilmore. "Our Early Authors." The XIX Century 1 (August 1869): 169-77; reprinted in Simms, Essays on the Literary and Intellectual History of South Carolina. Columbia: University of South Carolina, 1977. SCHS

Character sketches and anecdotes of the political and historical writers of the Revolutionary period in South Carolina. "Drayton and the Middletons lived in great splendor on the Ashley....Drayton Hall was famous throughout the country. Fabulous stories were told about its splendor, its grand halls, its glorious pictures, its stud of forty blooded horses of Arabian through English breeds, and these horses eating and drinking out of troughs of marble. These were exaggerations, but believed. The backwoodsmen and wagoner passing, peeped in with eager curiosity..." (p. 170 [p. 9 reprint]). Story of Gov. John Drayton's conversation with a wagoner at Drayton Hall (pp. 170-171 [pp. 9-10 reprint]). Other articles in the series (see succeeding issues of the magazine, or the reprint) describe writers in South Carolina up to about 1830.

Smith, D.E. Huger. "An Account of the Tattnall and Fenwick Families in South Carolina." South Carolina Historical and Genealogical Magazine 14 (January 1913): 1-19. CC, CCPL, CLS, SCHS

Notes on the early Draytons in South Carolina, specifically, whether there were one or two Thomas Draytons who immigrated and when he or they died (pp. 16-19). See also Taylor (Magazines and Journals, Part I), Drayton, J., Mayers and Drayton, T.D. Grimke (Manuscripts, Part I).

Smith, Henry A.M. "The Ashley River: Its Seats and Settlements." South Carolina Historical and Genealogical Magazine 20 (January and April 1919): 1-51, 75-122. CC, CCPL, CLS, SCHS

Drayton Hall: chain of title to the land, 1676-1820; description (pp. 91-94) by La Rochefoucault-Liancourt, 1796 (see Books, Part I); mention of "Drayton's seat" (p. 118) in Woodmason's poem, 1793 (see Magazines and Journals, Part I); description of Charles Hill's plantation (owned by John Drayton, 1760-77) across the river from Drayton Hall; mention of crops and outbuildings (pp. 10-12). Information on other Ashley River plantations up to the town of Old Dorchester.

_____. "Charleston and Charleston Neck." South Carolina Historical and Genealogical Magazine 19 (January 1918): 1-76. CC, CCPL, CLS, SCHS

Chain of title to 55 acres in the present city limits owned by John Drayton, 1746(?) (p. 14).

Figure 12: Chimneypiece, second floor great hall, 1956. Overmantel contains a painting on canvas depicting Drayton family coat of arms, accomplished sometime after 1885. (Samuel Chamberlain photograph)

Figure 13: Overmantel, first floor drawing room, 1956. (Samuel Chamberlain photograph)

_____. "Goose Creek." South Carolina Historical and Genealogi-
cal Magazine 29 (January 1928): 1-25. CC, CCPL, CLS, SCHS

Chain of title to about 450 acres on Goose Creek owned by Dr. Charles
Drayton from 1781 to 1819 (pp. 12-14).

Erratum: Charles Drayton apparently did not inherit Drayton Hall in
1779, but obtained the title from Rebecca, John Drayton's widow, in 1783.

_____. "The Upper Ashley; and the Mutations of Families."
South Carolina Historical and Genealogical Magazine 20 (July 1919): 151-98.
CC, CCPL, CLS, SCHS

Mention of Drayton property in Granville County and of Thomas Drayton's
expansion of Ashley River property. "Their present holdings are restricted
to the Drayton Hall property and a portion of Magnolia" (p. 194). Chains
of title and some descriptions for Ashley River plantations above Old
Dorchester (none owned by Draytons).

Taylor, Emily Heyward Drayton. "The Draytons of South Carolina and Phila-
delphia." Publications of the Genealogical Society of Pennsylvania 8
(March 1921): 1-26. Reprinted as a pamphlet under the title, Some
Account of the Draytons of South Carolina and Philadelphia, edited by
M. Atherton Leach. Lancaster, Pa.: Wickersham Press, 1921. CLS, SCHS

A genealogy of the Draytons, with biographical sketches of the most important members, including John, builder of Drayton Hall. Paragraphs on
most members of the family.

Errata: "John Drayton...born...circa 1712; died at his plantation, called
Strawberry, 34 May, 1779" (p. 9). John, Drayton Hall builder, was born
between 1714 and 1716; he died at Strawberry Ferry on the Cooper River,
not at a "plantation called Strawberry." Several other statements are
questionable (see Drayton, J., Mayers and Drayton, T.D. Grimke, Manuscripts, Part I).

Webber, Mabel L., ed. "Register of St. Andrews Parish, Berkeley County, S.C.,
1719-1774." South Carolina Historical and Genealogical Magazine 12
(October 1911); 15 (April 1914). CC, CCPL, CLS, SCHS

Includes dates of births, deaths and marriages of the Drayton family.

Wilson, John. "Lieutenant John Wilson's 'Journal of the Siege of Charleston'."
Edited by Joseph I. Waring. South Carolina Historical Magazine 66 (July
1965): 175-82. CC, CCPL, CLS, SCHS

"Tuesday, March 28, [1780] about 12 o'clock the Army advanced to
Drayton's House & halted during the Night when the Flat Boats moved

to Drayton's Landing," (p. 178). The editor identifies "Drayton's House" as Drayton Hall. "Wednesday, March 29, about 8 P.M. the army crossed Ashley River & landed at Fowler's Plantation about 14 miles from Charles-Town," (ibid.).

Errata: "Fowler's" is Fuller's. "About 8 P.M." The diaries of two Hessian officers place the crossing early in the morning; Wilson may have written "8 P.M." when he meant "8 A.M." (See Uhlendorf, Books, Part I, pp. 33, 223.)

C.W. [Charles Woodmason] "C.W. in Carolina to E.J. at Gosport." The Gentleman's Magazine, July 1753, pp. 337-38. CLS

A "poetical essay" praising the refinement of South Carolina plantation life, but expressing a longing for England. (This passage is quoted in several sources, including Page, see Books, Part I, and Smith, H., Magazines and Journals, Part I.) "...here Drayton's seat and Middleton's is found Delightful villa's! be they long renown'd" (p. 338). Footnote to identify these names: "Gentlemen of large estates in Goose Creek, who have superb seats that would make a good figure in England."

Uncorroborated statement: John Drayton is not known to have had an estate on Goose Creek.

Woolson, Constance Fenimore. "Up the Ashley and Cooper." Harper's New Monthly Magazine, December 1875, pp. 1-24. CC, CLS, SCHS

Important description of Drayton Hall: "...the only one of these old homes now remaining, was built in 1740 by Thomas Drayton, Esq., and named after the family residence, Drayton Hall, Northamptonshire, England; its cost at that early period being ninety thousand dollars." "...the fireplaces are adorned with colored tiles." "In one of the cellars are to be seen a number of marble columns lying on the ground just as they came from England. These columns have given rise to the story that the old mansion was never entirely finished; but this is an error, the columns having been intended not for the house, but for a gateway outside" (pp. 4-6). Other plantations in the area mentioned as well. Illustrations of river and land facades of the house and portrait of Wm. Henry Drayton.

"At the close of the late war, when every other mansion in this parish was burned, Drayton Hall was spared. It is said that a negro declared that its owner was a Union man, which story had so much foundation in fact as this: A Northern Drayton, a near relative of the South Carolina family, was actually outside the bar with the fleet which had so long blockaded Charleston Harbor; this was Captain Percival Drayton, of the United States navy...." (pp. 5-6).

Phosphate industry: "...the trenches of the mines are invading the

grounds of our old plantations. At Drayton Hall children run after the
visitors to sell 'sharks' teeth'. One of these teeth weighed two pounds
and a quarter, and measured six inches from tip to tip" (p. 24).

Errata: "...built...by Thomas Drayton, Esq.", actually by John. "Much of
the finer material having been imported from England." National Trust
for Historic Preservation architectural study indicates that probably
only the columns, fireplace tiles and marble fireplace surrounds were
imported. "The stairway, the mantels, and the wainscot...are of solid
mahogany...the wainscot at a later period having been painted over."
Only the balusters and some small decorative elements are mahogany.
The rest of the woodwork is almost all cypress, which was probably
painted at an early date. "Drayton Hall, the only one of these old
homes now remaining." Two antebellum houses on the north bank of the
Ashley survived the War Between the States, but one (Archdale Hall) was
destroyed by the 1886 earthquake, and the other (Jeny's) burned in the
early 1900s. Drayton Hall was the only survivor in St. Andrew's Parish
on the west bank. "Kitchens and ovens below." The kitchen was apparently
on the ground floor, but there is no evidence of an oven in the main
house; the ovens were presumably in one of the flankers.

Uncorroborated statements: "They came to the province in 1671." There
is no documentation for arrival before 1679, although Gov. John Drayton
said it was 1671. "...its cost...being ninety thousand dollars."
This article is the earliest known reference to the cost. "These columns
have given rise to the story that the old mansion was never entirely
finished."   The earliest known version of this story is in an 1860
newspaper article, "St. Andrew's Parish" (see Newspapers, Part I),
which does not mention the columns. "The columns...intended...for a
gateway outside." This is the earliest known reference, both to the
columns and to their intended use. "Carpets...at both entrances and
out to the carriageways." This implies that there were driveways on
both fronts of the house, which has not been substantiated. "Cornwallis
occupied Drayton Hall as his headquarters during portions of the years
1780 and 1781, appointing receivers for the estate." Cornwallis was
in the Charleston area for only a few months in 1780 and not at all in
1781. The only time it is relatively certain that he was at Drayton
Hall is on 28-29 March 1780 (see Uhlendorf, Books, Part I); Clinton
and Wilson, Magazines and Journals, Part I). There is no known record
of the British "appointing receivers for the estate."

"The letters 'K.W.' are still to be seen cut into one of the bricks."
No one today can find these initials. This story is often repeated,
but almost every writer has a different idea of the location of the
initials. "A negro declared that its owner was a Union man." This
is the earliest story of how the house was saved, but no positive
proof has been found. "A Northern Drayton...was actually outside the
bar." Captain Percival Drayton was in the blockading fleet off Charleston from 1861 to 1863, but after that was transferred to the Gulf of
Mexico; there is no known evidence of his return to the South Atlantic

squadron. (Charleston fell in February 1865, and the Ashley River plantations were plundered about the same time.)

NEWSPAPERS

W.S.B. [William Shaw Bowen]   "Drayton Hall and Magnolia Gardens." Providence Journal, 4 April 1885. SCHS

Important description of Drayton Hall: "Ancient Drayton Hall...is undoubtedly one of the best specimens of a manorial residence in the United States. Before the civil war Drayton Hall was surrounded by a garden as rare as that of Magnolia....The space between the river and the rear of the mansion was a thicket of azaleas and camelias and the broad lawn in front, dotted with live oaks and flanking the main carriage way for half a mile to the Charleston road, must have resembled the grounds of an English nobleman."

The article says that the grounds were devastated during the war and that the house was occupied by freedmen when the owner, Charles H. Drayton IV, returned. "Exactly why the house was spared from burning when all other estates, far and near, were given over to the torch, the owner does not understand." The author gives two possible reasons why the house was spared; because "Commodore Percival Drayton, of the United States Navy, was of the family," or because the soldiers were impressed by the house. "Prior to the recent reoccupancy of the hall by Col. Drayton, vandal sight-seers with the inherent proneness of Americans to obtain 'relics' – cleaned out the tiles and even pulled off some of the carved festoons from the wainscot....The basement is occupied by servants' quarters and two brick buildings flanking the entrance were formerly the abiding places of the house servants....The cultivation of Sea Island cotton has been abandoned and the fortunate discovery of immense beds of natural phosphate rock on the estate is rapidly restoring the shattered fortunes of the owner....The restoration of Drayton Hall is already mapped out and before many years have lapsed the old mansion will shine forth resplendent with original beauty and completeness." The article also treats Revolutionary War stories connected with the house.

Errata: "...the seat of eight generations of the Drayton family." Six generations, at the most, up to 1885. "...the former slaves of the Draytons...numbering many hundreds." Chalmers Davidson's research (see Books, Part I) indicates that there were fewer than 100 slaves at Drayton Hall in 1860. "The second story is similar to the first, while the third lacks the large central hall." There is no third story. In local usage the first floor is called the ground floor, thus there would be only two stories. "...oaken floors." The floors are pine.

Uncorroborated statements: Neither of the stories of why the house was spared has been documented. The stories of the house in the Revolution are also uncorroborated.

"Drayton Hall Not Victim of Neglect, Brothers Say." Charleston News and Courier, 5 December 1972, p. 10A. CC, CCPL, CLS

Charles H. and Francis B. Drayton, owners of the house, respond to accusations that the house is endangered by neglect.

"Drayton Hall Preservation Appeal Made." Charleston Evening Post, 9 March 1973, p. 2A. CCPL, CLS

Letitia Galbraith of the National Trust for Historic Preservation, speaking in Charleston, urges preservation of the environment as well as of the house and grounds.

"J.V.N., Jr." "Do You Know Your Charleston? - Drayton Hall." Charleston News and Courier, 2 May 1938, p. 10. CC, CCPL, CLS

Brief history of the house, with an unusually detailed story of how the house was saved in 1865.

Erratum: Thomas Drayton, not John Drayton, is stated to be the builder.

Laurens, Henry [Comus]. Article in South Carolina and American General Gazette, 30 April 1779. CLS

Criticizes and satirizes William Henry Drayton's response to a speech by King George III.

"Lease is Signed for Drayton Hall." Charleston Evening Post, 3 January 1973, p. 1A. CCPL, CLS

National Trust for Historic Preservation and Historic Charleston Foundation lease the house and surrounding property. Photograph of land front.

"Mechanicks of the Committee." Letter in South-Carolina Gazette, 5 October 1769, p. 1. CCPL, CLS

Attacks William Henry Drayton's opposition to nonimportation (i.e., the "mechanicks" supporting nonimportation), and his alleged contempt for those without "a liberal education."

Miller, Gardner B. "Drayton Hall Dedicated as Landmark." Charleston News and Courier, 27 May 1976, p. 10B. CC, CCPL, CLS

Drayton Hall becomes a National Historic Landmark. Photograph.

"National Landmark." Charleston Evening Post, 26 May 1976, p. 1A. CCPL, CLS

Drayton Hall becomes a National Historic Landmark.

I. NEWSPAPERS

"National Landmark." Editorial in Charleston Evening Post, 31 May 1976, p.
6A. CCPL, CLS

Praise of Dr. Ernest A. Connally's speech on architecture, builders.
Support of a plan to safeguard Drayton Hall against urban sprawl.

"Phosphate Industry Once Reigned on Ashley." Charleston News and Courier,
5 May 1974, p. 1E. CC, CCPL, CLS

Describes mining at Drayton Hall after the War Between the States.
Photograph of a mine train at Drayton Hall.

"Preservation Groups Take Option on Drayton Hall." Charleston News and
Courier, 4 January 1973, p. 1A. CC, CCPL, CLS

National Trust for Historic Preservation and Historic Charleston Foundation lease the house with option to buy it. Photographs of the ceremony
and the land front of the house.

South Carolina and American General Gazette, 9 April 1779. CLS

Advertisement of a horse at stud at Drayton Hall: "PHARAOH will cover
this season at Drayton Hall, Fifty Pounds each mare...."

"South Carolina Birthday." Charleston News and Courier, 30 Dec. 1946, p. 4.
CC, CCPL, CLS

Biographical sketch of Col. William Drayton (1776-1846). For more information see Dictionary of American Biography.

"South Carolina Birthday." Charleston News and Courier, 21 March 1947, p. 4.
CC, CCPL, CLS

Biographical sketch of Judge William Drayton (1732-90). For more information see Dictionary of American Biography.

South-Carolina Gazette, 22 December 1758. CCPL, CLS

Advertisement for Dr. Charles Hill's plantation across the river from
Drayton Hall, describing Hill's crops, house and outbuildings, and men-
tioning the view of "John Drayton Esqr's Palace and Gardens."

"St. Andrew's Parish." New York Spirit of the Times, 7 April 1860; reprinted
in Charleston Mercury, 10 April 1860, p. 4. CC, CCPL, CLS

"Drayton Hall...is a model piece of architecture, and the most costly
private home probably in the United States." Story that the house was
built so that a Miss Middleton would marry John Drayton. "...the ser-

46

vants' hall and the kitchen, fine buildings to the right and left of the mansion, were never completed. Until within a few years the property has been neglected - the garden is lost to view, being covered with weeds or planted in cotton; the kitchen has fallen into decay from neglect, and the old mansion itself has been sadly misused....We believe it is the intention of the present owner to restore everything, as nearly as possible, to its original perfection, and workmen are now busy in restoring the building and grounds."

Errata: "...now in possession of Dr. John Drayton." Other evidence indicates that the actual owner was John's nephew, Charles Henry Drayton IV (2nd great-grandson of John, Drayton Hall builder) although Dr. John Drayton appears to have had charge of the property until after the War Between the States. "...oaken floors." Actually pine. "John Drayton... having buried his third wife, courted...a Miss Middleton." His fourth wife was Rebecca Perry; none of his wives was a Middleton. The house could not have been built for his fourth wife, since his third wife died in 1772, some 30 years after the house was finished. (It could conceivably have been built for his second wife, Charlotta Bull, whom he married in 1741.)

Uncorroborated statement: "...the servants' hall and the kitchen...were never completed." The flankers were complete enough to be used for many years. Perhaps the article means that they were not completed according to the original plan. (There is an existing design, that resembles Drayton Hall, showing flankers much larger than those built.)

Stockton, Robert P. "Drayton Hall Remains as Lasting Landmark." <u>Charleston News and Courier</u>, 22 April 1974, p. 1B. CC, CCPL, CLS

Summary of the historical and architectural importance of the house.

Stockton, Robert. "Drayton Hall Future Undecided." <u>Charleston News and Courier</u>, 12 April 1976, p. 1B. CC, CCPL, CLS

Describes work of the archaeologist, historical architect and architectural historian. 1875 engraving of river front.

_____. "Landmark's Environment Important." <u>Charleston News and Courier</u>, 9 March 1973, p. 1B. CC, CCPL, CLS

Coverage of Galbraith speech. (See "Drayton Hall Preservation Appeal Made," Newspapers, Part I.)

"$2 million asked for Restoration of Drayton Hall." <u>Charleston Evening Post</u>, 23 September 1974, p. 1B. CCPL, CLS

National Trust for Historic Preservation begins drive to raise funds for preservation of the house and for an endowment fund for long-range use.

Figure 14: Train carrying phosphate, ca. 1900. The presence of phosphate (used as fertilizer) at Drayton Hall is mentioned in writings as early as 1848. After the War Between the States and until about 1915, phosphate mining was the principal economic activity at Drayton Hall. (William P. Dowling photograph—photocopy courtesy of Historic Charleston Foundation)

Figure 15: View toward the Ashley River, ca. 1900. (Photocopy courtesy of Historic Charleston Foundation)

Figure 16: Live oak, land side, ca. 1900. The lawn is dotted with live oaks, which also line the drive from the Ashley River Road. This magnificent specimen, which is still standing, is the oldest live oak at Drayton Hall. (William P. Dowling photograph--photocopy courtesy of Historic Charleston Foundation)

Figure 17: Ornamental pond between land facade and Ashley River Road, ca. 1900. The live oaks on the bank are still standing. (William P. Dowling photograph--photocopy courtesy of Historic Charleston Foundation)

I. NEWSPAPERS

Wallace, Sue. "Architects Draw from Past for Future." Charleston News and
    Courier, 25 August 1974, p. 1C. CC, CCPL, CLS

    Describes work of the Historic American Buildings Survey at Drayton Hall.
    Several detailed measured drawings of interior and river front.

MANUSCRIPTS

Davis, Jefferson, to Gen. Thomas F. Drayton, 27 January 1886. Typed copy in
    Drayton Folder, South Carolina File. SCHS

    Deals with labor problems., family news, Drayton's daughter's plans to
    visit Davis. No mention of the Draytons of Drayton Hall.

Drayton, Charlotta, Copy Books, nos. 1 and 2, ca. 1923. Typed copy.
    SCHS

    A copy of Gov. John Drayton's "History and Genealogy of the Drayton
    Family," 1817. Some editorial notes by Charles Drayton III (great-
    grandson of John, Drayton Hall builder), and possibly by Charles
    Drayton IV (second great-grandson) and Charlotta Drayton (third
    great-granddaughter).

    _____ Copy Book, no. 3, ca. 1923. Typed copy. SCHS

    Charles Drayton III's copies of a letter from Stephen Drayton to Charles
    Drayton I (n.d.) regarding history of Draytons in England; The Hon.
    John Drayton's reasons "why I made my will as I have done," 8 April
    1767; notes on Drayton coats of arms; defense of the Hon. John Drayton's
    character and actions by Charles Drayton III; detailed genealogy of
    several branches of the family from Thomas the immigrant to Charles
    Henry Drayton VI (1918); sometimes incorrect.

    _____ Copy Books, nos. 4 and 5, 1924. Typed copy. SCHS

    Copies of letters from Charles Drayton II and Mary Middleton Drayton
    to their son Charles III, 1833-36. Consists of family news and advice.

"Drayton" [Coats of Arms]. Typed note in Drayton Folder, South Carolina File,
    SCHS

    Note on coats of arms in which Gov. John Drayton clears up confusion be-
    tween the personal coat of arms of the poet Michael Drayton and the family
    coat of arms. (See illustrations of coats of arms in Drayton, J. and
    Drayton, C., Manuscripts, Part I.)

Drayton, [Dr.] John, to Mr. and Mrs. James S. Gibbes, 20 December 1872. James
    Shoolbred Gibbes Correspondence. CLS

The son of Charles Drayton II, and great-grandson of John, Drayton Hall
builder, John Drayton, "wandering over the world," writes from Galveston
to congratulate his Gibbes cousins on the wedding of their daughter and
gives his love to the family.

Drayton, Eliza (daughter of Glen Drayton, granddaughter of John, Drayton Hall
    builder) to Mrs. Carns, 4 March 1794. SCHS

(Noted as being written from "Ashley.") Encloses a pseudo-biblical text
to be worn as a "Charm for the fever & Ague" by Mrs. Carns's son.

Drayton, [Gov.] John. "History and Genealogy of the Drayton Family," 1817.
    SCHS

South Carolina Historical Society has three copies. One (ms volume)
extensively annotated by Charles Drayton III (1847) and by "M.G.D."
(identity undetermined, ca. 1900); one (microfilmed, 1847?) with list
of birth and death dates appended by M.G.D.; and one manuscript with
only Charles Drayton III's annotation. History goes back to 1066 and
includes descriptions of Drayton House, Northamptonshire, England; the
first house at Magnolia; and Drayton Hall. "[John Drayton] erected...a
Mansion-House and other offices and buildings of Brick, which he named
Drayton Hall....Great attention and expense was bestowed on this building...and it is finished on so large a scale, and in so elegant a style,
that to this day there is no [other] such building in the State of South
Carolina; whether public or private. The gardens connected with it are
laid out in appropriate style after the English mode of Gardening, and
by an English Gardener." The section dealing with John, Drayton Hall
builder, and his descendants is printed with Gov. John Drayton's Carolinian Florist (see Books, Part I). The author's account of John, Drayton
Hall builder, should be used with caution because the governor was notice-
ably bitter that his father, William Henry, did not inherit Drayton Hall.

Errata: "[At Drayton Hall] all [John Drayton's] children were born."
Two children were born before Drayton Hall was begun, but died in infancy.
All of John's surviving children were born at Drayton Hall. "The above
seat of Magnolia has always been in the Drayton Family." Thomas Drayton
obtained the land from Stephen Fox between 1696 and 1717. Perhaps the
writer means the house, not the land.

Uncorroborated statements: "[Thomas Drayton] came here...from Barbadoes,
about the year 1671." There is no documentation for his arrival before
1679.

_____ to Daniel Huger, 10 December 1808. CLS, SCHS

Brief note notifying Huger of his appointment as Drayton's private secretary.

_____ to Robert Smith, 16 November 1810. CLS

Deals with legal matters: efforts of the heirs of John Rudolph Faesch [?] to obtain title to an estate in Switzerland. Nothing on the Drayton family.

Drayton, John Edward, to Percival Drayton, 28 June 1865. Typed copy in Drayton Folder. SCHS

Son of Gen. Thomas F. Drayton (CSA) writes to his uncle, Percival Drayton (USN), giving news of the immediate family conditions at the end of the War Between the States and hopes for the future. John Edward Drayton's plantation, Fish Hall, on Hilton Head Island has been sold for taxes. No mention of Drayton Hall.

Drayton, Maria Henrietta. "Commonplace Book." (Late 18th century, early 19th century) Gibbes-Gilchrist Collection. SCHS

Passages copied from books and magazines on useful and educational subjects, by a daughter of the first Dr. Charles Drayton of Drayton Hall.

Drayton, S[arah?] M[otte?], to Samuel Prioleau, 15 September 1826 and 12 May 1829. Old Manuscripts (Miscellaneous) Collection, Rare Book Room. CC

Sarah Motte Drayton, possible writer of this letter, was a daughter of Judge William Drayton, and grandniece of John, Drayton Hall builder. Letters from residence in Northampton, Mass., dealing with visitors from Charleston, family news (no mention of Drayton Hall), problems with rental of a house on Church Street, Charleston.

Drayton, Theodore D. Grimke. "Drayton Genealogy." Typed copy in Drayton Folder, South Carolina File. SCHS

Extracts from various source books and manuscripts by a grandson of the Hon. John Drayton and brother of John Grimke Drayton, and a complete genealogy of the American branch of the family from 1679 to 1888, with additional notes from the 1960s.

Drayton, Thomas F., to Lewis R. Gibbes, 24 May 1879. Lewis R. Gibbes Papers, vol. 11. Originals in Library of Congress, microfilm at CC.

Reply to a request for information on Drayton family history, enclosing a family tree (missing) and advising Gibbes to contact William Drayton in Philadelphia for further information.

Drayton, William, to Maj. Gen. [Nathanael] Green[e], 7 February 1785. SCHS

Brief note enclosed with opinions on legal cases. No family information.

_____ to J.R. Poinsett and D.E. Huger, 1832-33. Originals
at Historical Society of Pennsylvania. Transcripts in Drayton Folder,
South Carolina File. SCHS

Letters dealing with politics: the tariff, nullification of tariff,
appointment of South Carolinians to office.

FitzSimons, Mrs. Waveland. "Drayton Folder." FitzSimons Genealogical Collection. SCHS

Consists of notes on the children of Thomas Drayton, including the
Hon. John Drayton, builder of Drayton Hall. Note: Other sources give
John Drayton's mother's name as Anne Fox, not Elizabeth Fox as in this
source.

Gibbes, James S., (first cousin of Lewis R. Gibbes) to Mary Evans, 14 April
1842. James Shoolbred Gibbes Correspondence. CLS

Mentions Eleanor Gibbes's visit to Drayton Hall with Charles Drayton
(III).

Gibbes, Lewis R., (son of Maria Henrietta Drayton and Lewis L. Gibbes; great-
grandson of John Drayton, Drayton Hall builder) to Miss H[enrietta].
A[ugusta]. Drayton, (granddaughter of John, Drayton Hall builder) 8 May
1837. Gibbes-Gilchrist Papers. SCHS

Mentions the fact that none of the family is "permanently fixed excepting
Charles' family" [at Drayton Hall]. Some other family news; not clear
whether it refers to Gibbeses or Draytons. "Report of John's [Dr. John
Drayton's?] engagement...."

_____ to Miss H[enrietta]. A[ugusta]. Drayton (in Philadelphia), 1 July 1837. Gibbes-Gilchrist Papers. SCHS

Gibbes mentions "the state of distress in which John and Charles are....
John certainly has my consent to do with the estate whatever he can to
save himself...as the possession of it has been productive of little
benefit and less pleasure to us." John owes Gibbes "between 6 and 7
hundred dollars." (John and Charles have not been identified; perhaps
John Grimke Drayton and Charles Drayton III, great-grandsons of John,
Drayton Hall builder.)

Gibbes, Maria Henrietta Drayton, to Lewis L. Gibbes, 28 May [ca. 1815].
Gibbes-Gilchrist papers. SCHS

The writer and her son, Lewis R. Gibbes, are visiting at Drayton Hall.
Mention of several of the Draytons: Henrietta (Augusta, daughter of
Charles I), Charles (II) and Mary (Shoolbred, his wife).

I. MANUSCRIPTS

Kaminer, Gulielma Melton. "A Dictionary of South Carolina Biography during the Period of the Royal Government (1719-1776)." Masters thesis, University of South Carolina, 1926. CLS

Includes biographical sketches of the Hon. John Drayton, Drayton Hall builder, and William Henry Drayton. Brief entry for John Drayton, focusing on his political career. More information in the William Henry Drayton entry, but see Dabney and Dargan (Books, Part I) for a fuller treatment.

Laurens, Henry. Journal [account book], 1766-73. Microfilm. CC

Monetary transactions involving Hon. John Drayton, 31 December 1767, 17 March 1768; William Drayton, 5 November 1767, 11 March 1768; William Henry Drayton, (purchase of 276 12-inch tiles), 22 November 1767.

Le Conte, John, to Lewis R. Gibbes, 10 April 1865. Lewis R. Gibbes Papers, vol. 9. Originals in Library of Congress, microfilm at CC.

"Mrs. Drayton's beautiful writing-desk," which Gibbes had left in Le Conte's care, was captured by Sherman's troops with other furniture being sent out of Columbia.

Mayers, J. Alex. "De Vere of Drayton Genealogy." Typescript in Drayton Folder, South Carolina File. SCHS

Genealogy from Alberic de Vere (?-1088) to Thomas (c. 1625-1702), father of the Thomas who immigrated to South Carolina, and tracing the Barbados branch of the family to 1901. Additional information (entitled "Data: Drayton Genealogy"): extracts of references to Drayton in English records, 1242-1645.

Mellichamp, J.H., to Lewis R. Gibbes, 11 March 1864. Lewis R. Gibbes Papers, vol. 9. Originals in Library of Congress, microfilm at CC.

Mentions "Miss Anna Drayton's" (probably Anna Maria, daughter of Gen. Thomas F. Drayton) request for botanical specimens for Gibbes.

Plats. H.A.M. Smith Collection. SCHS

Includes plans of "a body of land in St. Andrew's Parish...belonging to Charles Drayton" (1790), "Drayton's Cowpen Plantation, estate of John Drayton, St. Paul's Parish" (n.d.), "Part of Drayton's Cowpen conveyed to William Washington, March 26, 1796."

Quinn, Mrs. John. "Genealogy of the Lewis Ladson Gibbes - Maria Henrietta Drayton Family." Typescript. SCHS

Information on the Gibbes descendants of a daughter of Dr. Charles Drayton I, of Drayton Hall.

Read, Motte Alston. "Tatnall, Fenwick, Drayton Folder." Read Genealogical
Collection. SCHS

Contains notes on the first Drayton in America (published in Smith, D.E.H.,
[see Magazines and Journals, Part I]) and a genealogical table of the first
four generations of South Carolina Draytons, "compiled from an old family
record." (Gov. John Drayton's "History and Genealogy"?)

Smith, Robert. Account Book, 1788-1801. Microfilm, CC.

By the principal of the College of Charleston. Transactions involving
Jacob Drayton (son of Judge William Drayton) 5 September 1794, and John
Drayton (son of Wm. Henry) 6 November 1794.

Stone, Anna Drayton Thomas, to David McC. Wright, 13 July 1961. Letter in
Pope File. SCHS

The writer seeks to refute statements in Holmgren (see Books, Part I)
dealing with Drayton land holdings on the island. Stone's opinions seem
to be well documented.

Van Ravenswaay, Charles, to Anna Wells Rutledge, 17 February 1969. Letter in
Drayton Folder, South Carolina File. SCHS

Deals with Drayton papers and portraits in England.

Webber, Mabel L.C. "Drayton Folder," Webber Genealogical Collection, SCHS.

Miscellaneous primary source notes on the Draytons. Mostly births,
marriages, deaths from St. Andrew's Parish register and lists of rela-
tives from wills in Charleston County will books.

Figure 18: Land facade, ca. 1900. At times as many as 100 sheep were kept at Drayton Hall and were used to crop the lawn. (Photocopy courtesy of Historic Charleston Foundation)

PART II

BACKGROUND MATERIAL

BOOKS

Burke, Edmund. An Account of the European Settlements in America. 2 vols.
5th ed. London: J. Dodsley, 1770. CC, CLS

Volume 2 contains description of "Situation, climate, etc. of Carolina.
Its animal and vegetable productions;" also rice and indigo cultivation;
Charlestown lifestyle (pp. 241-60).

Burton, E. Milby. South Carolina Silversmiths 1690-1860. Charleston: The
Charleston Museum, 1968. CC, CCPL, CLS, SCHS

Good information on silverware made in South Carolina.

The Charleston Book: A Miscellany in Prose and Verse. Charleston: Samuel
Hart, 1845. SCHS

Collection of writings by 19th-century Charlestonians; gives some indica-
tion of the type of writing admired in the antebellum low country.

Crèvecoeur, Michel Guillaume St. Jean de [J. Hector St. John]. Letters from
an American Farmer. London: 1782. CC, CCPL

Criticism of the luxury and refinement of Charles Town (pp. 213-216).

Curtis, Elizabeth Gibbon. Gateways and Doorways of Charleston, South Carolina
in the Eighteenth and the Nineteenth Centuries. New York: Architectural
Book Publishing Co., 1926. CCPL, CLS

Photographs and captions of Charleston gates and doors.

Devereux, Anthony Q. The Rice Princes: A Rice Epoch Revisited. Columbia, S.C.:
State Printing Co., 1973. CC, CCPL, CLS, SCHS

Deals with planter families of the Georgetown area.

Ellet, Elizabeth F. The Queens of American Society. Third ed. New York:
Charles Scribner & Co., 1868. CLS, SCHS

Stories of Charleston ladies and society in the Revolutionary War period
(pp. 181-93).

II. BOOKS

Elzas, Barnett A. <u>Leaves from My Historical Scrap Book</u>. Charleston: 1907–08. CCPL, CLS, SCHS

    A miscellany of information on the history of the Charleston area, including useful lists of newspaper articles on various topics.

Field, Horace, and Bunney, Michael. <u>English Domestic Architecture of the XVII and XVIII Centuries</u>. London: G. Bell & Sons, 1928. CLS

    Measured drawings, photographs and descriptions of the manor houses, town houses and public buildings of the era when Drayton Hall was built.

Fraser, Charles. <u>A Charleston Sketchbook, 1796–1806</u>. Rutland, Vt.: Charles E. Tuttle Co., 1959. CLS, SCHS

    Paintings of buildings in the Charleston area, including a number of plantations.

French, Mrs. A.M. <u>Slavery in South Carolina and the Ex-Slaves</u>. New York: Winchell M. French, 1862. CC, CLS

    Description of slavery and efforts to educate ex-slaves at Union-held Port Royal. Written by a fervent abolitionist.

Genovese, Eugene D. <u>Roll, Jordan, Roll: The World the Slaves Made</u>. New York: Pantheon Books, 1974. CC, CCPL, CLS

    Slavery from the slave's point of view and the distinctive culture of the slaves. Mostly from 19th-century sources.

Gotch, J. Alfred. <u>Inigo Jones</u>. London: Methuen & Co., 1928. CLS

    Biography of the 17th-century English architect whose designs influenced Drayton Hall's architect. Designs for the Banqueting House, Whitehall [London], bearing a certain resemblance to Drayton Hall (pp. 101–107).

Halfpenny, William. <u>Practical Architecture or A Sure Guide to the True Working According to the Rules of that Science</u>. London: 1730; reprinted, New York: Benjamin Blom, Inc., 1970. CC

    A handbook that could have been used by the architect of Drayton Hall. Consists of drawings of columns, doors and windows, chiefly from Inigo Jones and Palladio, with tables of proportions for each item.

Hewatt, Alexander. <u>An Historical Account of the Rise and Progress of the Colonies of South Carolina and Georgia</u>. 2 vols. London: 1779; reprinted, Spartanburg, S.C.: The Reprint Co., 1971. CC, CLS, SCHS

    Mainly a political history, but some descriptive passages in volume II:

58

Climate, health, indigo cultivation (pp. 134-145); wild and cultivated plants (pp. 206-208); description of Charles Town and its way of life (pp. 288-307).

Heyward, Duncan Clinch. <u>Seed from Madagascar</u>. Chapel Hill: University of North Carolina Press, 1937. CC, CCPL, CLS, SCHS

Deals with the Heyward family and their life on a South Carolina rice plantation.

Hussy, Christopher. <u>English Country Houses: Early Georgian, 1715-1760</u>. London: Country Life, 1955. CLS

Introduction to the Palladian style (that of Drayton Hall) and the English architects who followed that style (pp. 18-23). Examples of Palladian houses in England, including plans; exterior and interior photographs, several of which show some similarities to Drayton Hall.

Kemble, Frances Anne. <u>Journal of a Residence on a Georgian Plantation in 1838-1839</u>. New York: Harper & Brothers, 1864; reprinted, Chicago: Afro-American Press, 1969. CC, CLS

Plantation life in coastal Georgia was very similar to that in coastal South Carolina and this is one of the best eyewitness accounts of the slave plantation in operation. Written by an abolitionist; not propagandistic.

Langley, Batty, and Langley, Thomas. <u>The Builders Jewel: or the Youth's Instructor, & Workman's Rememberancer</u>. London: 1746; reprinted, New York: Benjamin Blom, Inc., 1970. CC

Illustrations and rules of proportions for columns, cornices, rafters, pediments, etc., as used in English architecture contemporary with Drayton Hall.

Leighton, Ann. <u>American Gardens in the Eighteenth Century: "For Use or for Delight."</u> Boston: Houghton Mifflin Co., 1976. CCPL

English gardens of the period (pp. 325-59); general description of plantation gardens (pp. 365-67); gardens of the Charleston area (pp. 379-81).

Martineau, Harriet. <u>Retrospect of Western Travel</u>. 2 vols. London: Saunders & Otley, 1838. CC, CLS

Volume 1: Daily life on a cotton plantation described (pp. 214-223). Impressions of Charleston: hospitality, politics, views on slavery (pp. 223-241).

Mazyck, Arthur. <u>Guide to Charleston, Illustrated</u>. Charleston: Walker, Evans & Cogswell, 1875. CCPL, CLS, SCHS

Discusses phosphate mining (pp. 161-165).

Moreau de Saint-Mery, Mederic-Louis-Elie. Moreau de St. Mery's American
   Journey. Edited by Kenneth Roberts and Anna M. Roberts. Garden City,
   New York: Doubleday & Co., 1947. CC, CCPL, CLS

   A French traveler's impressions of the United States in the 1790s.
   Several mentions of slavery, fires, climate in Charleston.

Morris, Robert. Lectures on Architecture: Consisting of Rules Founded Upon
   Harmonick and Arithmetical Proportions in Building.... London: J.
   Brindley, 1734. CC, CLS

   Observations on the 18th-century philosophy of architecture; which order
   of architecture is suited to a certain site; rules for proportions; notes
   on stairs, outbuildings, porticoes, etc. Few illustrations. (Note: The
   copy in the Charleston Library Society was owned in 1802 by Charleston
   architect Gabriel Manigault.)

Pain, William. The Builder's Companion: Demonstrating All the Principal
   Rules of Architecture. London: 1762; reprinted in The Monograph Series:
   Recording the Architecture of the American Colonies & the Early Republic,
   Vol. XVII (1931) Nos. 1 and 2. CC (No. 2 only)

   Drawings with detailed measurements for columns, doors, windows, pediments, gateposts, pedestals, moldings, mantels, stairways, etc., of a
   period slightly later than Drayton Hall but illustrating the same principles of design.

Phillips, Ulrich B., ed. Plantation and Frontier Documents: 1649-1863. 2
   vols. Cleveland: Arthur H. Clark Co., 1909. CC, CLS, SCHS

   Includes documents illustrating life on several coastal plantations
   in South Carolina and Georgia. Contracts, instructions to managers,
   expense records, advertisements, letters, etc.

Pickering, Ernest. The Homes of America. New York: Thomas Y. Crowell, 1951.
   CLS

   Photographs and descriptions of several historic houses in the Charleston
   area.

Pinckney, Elise. Thomas and Elizabeth Lamboll: Early Charleston Gardeners.
   Charleston: The Charleston Museum, 1969. CC, CCPL, CLS, SCHS

   Includes useful general information on gardening in colonial South
   Carolina; mention of types of plants used, etc.

Porter, A. Toomer. Led On! Step by Step. New York: G.P. Putnam's Sons,
   1898; reprinted, New York: Arno Press, 1967. CC, CCPL, CLS, SCHS

Autobiography of a Charleston clergyman and educator. Description of plantation life near Georgetown, 1830-51 (perhaps somewhat idealized) (pp. 12-80).

Power, Tyrone. Impressions of America during the Years 1833, 1834, and 1835. 2 vols. London: Richard Bently, 1836. CC, CLS

An English traveler's impression of Charleston (vol. 2): health of different social classes, decline of family fortunes and prevalence of "hereditary idlers" (pp. 93-101). "At this season [28 November 1834] Charleston is dull to a proverb, most of the planters, with their families, being in the country, and the rest preparing to follow; the city is, therefore, nearly abandoned to the cotton-shippers; and so it will remain until the month of February, when the race-meeting draws the whole State together; and, for a period of four or five weeks, few places, as I learn, can be more lively or more sociable" (pp. 94-95).

Prime, Alfred Coxe, ed. The Arts & Crafts in Philadelphia, Maryland and South Carolina. 2 vols. Topsfield, Mass.: The Walpole Society, 1929-33; reprinted, New York: Da Capo Press, 1969. CC, CCPL, CLS

Newspaper advertisements and notices of artists and craftsmen: house carpenters, plasterers, architects, painters, cabinetmakers, carvers, etc. Many in Charleston, some of whom could have worked on Drayton Hall. Volume 1: 1721-1785, volume 2: 1786-1800.

Ramsey, Stanley C. Inigo Jones. New York: Charles Scribner's Sons, 1924. CC, CLS

Biography of the 17th-century English architect whose designs influenced the architect of Drayton Hall. Text is briefer than Gotch's (see Books, Part II) but Ramsey's book has more photographs of Jones' work, including interior details.

Repton, Humphry. The Art of Landscape Gardening. Edited by John Nolen. Boston: Houghton, Mifflin & Co., 1907. CLS

Selections from two works (1795 and 1803) by an English landscape architect, illustrating the principles of landscaping and grounds planning that may have been used at Drayton Hall. La Rochefoucault-Liancourt's description (see Books, Part I) of Drayton Hall grounds in 1796 seems generally to fit these principles, and Gov. John Drayton mentions an English gardener.

Reynolds, James. Andrea Palladio and the Winged Device. New York: Creative Age Press, 1948 CLS

Illustrates the influence of the Palladian architectural style (that of Drayton Hall) throughout the Western world. Palladianism in America (pp. 279-301). It is surprising that Drayton Hall is not mentioned, but two examples in Charleston are noted.

II. BOOKS

Rutledge, Archibald. <u>God's Children</u>. Indianapolis: Bobbs-Merrill, 1947. CCPL, CLS

Life of the blacks on Hampton, a plantation between Charleston and George-town, in the early 20th century. Slightly patronizing and idealized view but mostly sympathetic toward life of blacks.

Schwaab, Eugene L., ed. <u>Travels in the Old South</u>. 2 vols. Lexington: University Press of Kentucky, 1973. CC, SCHS

Consists of reprints of 18th and 19th-century articles. "South-Carolina" by "G.M." (<u>New England Magazine</u>, September-October 1831) describes Charleston, the character of the people, and a "typical" sea-island plantation (vol. 1, pp. 231-41). "Sketches of South Carolina" (<u>Knickerbocker Magazine</u>, March, May and July, 1843) describes Christmas on a plantation near Georgetown and slavery in South Carolina (vol. 2, pp. 317-31). "An Englishman in South Carolina" (<u>Continental Monthly</u>, Vol. 2 1862-63) describes life on a sea-island plantation and attitudes of the planter at the time of secession--December 1860 (vol. 2, pp. 560-73).

Smith, Alice R. Huger, and Smith, D.E. Huger. <u>The Dwelling Houses of Charleston, South Carolina</u>. Philadelphia: J.B. Lippincott Co., 1917. CC, CCPL, CLS, SCHS

Information on building materials, etc., is generally applicable to Drayton Hall. See especially pp. 361-75 for detailed information on the building of Charles Pinckney's house, 1745-46; specifications, names of craftsmen, sources of materials.

Smith, William Roy. <u>South Carolina as a Royal Province, 1719-1776</u>. 1903: reprinted, Freeport, N.Y.: Books for Libraries Press, 1970. CC, CCPL, CLS

A brief treatment of the subject. See Sirmans for a more complete account of the period to 1763, and Dabney and Dargan, for the period 1763-76 (both, Books, Part I).

Stampp, Kenneth M. <u>The Peculiar Institution: Slavery in the Ante-Bellum South</u>. New York: Alfred A. Knopf, 1956. CC, CCPL, CLS

An overview of slavery, with some specific references to South Carolina.

Stoney, Samuel Gaillard. <u>This Is Charleston</u>. 3rd ed. Charleston: Carolina Art Association, 1970. CC, CLS

A catalogue of historic buildings in Charleston, average as well as out-standing, with hundreds of photographs. Useful in showing the total architectural environment of past eras in Charleston.

Whilden, William G. "Reminiscences of Old Charleston." Year Book, City of Charleston, 1896. Charleston: Lucas & Richardson, [1897], pp. 402-17. CCPL, CLS

Description of household furnishings in the early 19th century (p. 411-12).

Wilkinson, Eliza. Letters of Eliza Wilkinson. New York: Samuel Colman, 1839; reprinted, New York: Arno Press, 1969. CC, CCPL, CLS, SCHS

Letters written in 1779-81 dealing with a plantation family on Yonge's Island, S.C. Good account of the fears of patriots during the British invasion and occupation.

Williams, Henry Lionel, and Williams, Ottalie K. A Guide to Old American Houses 1700-1900. New York: A.S. Barnes & Co., 1962. CCPL

Plans and descriptions of Georgian period houses of Charleston (pp. 72-79). For more information on the architecture of the area, see Stoney and Simons (Books, Part I) and Smith (Books, Part II).

Winterbotham, William. An Historical, Geographical, Commercial and Philosophical View of the United States of America. 4 vols. First American ed. New York: John Reid, 1796. CLS

Description of Charleston, luxuries and recreations of the upper class, uneasiness with slavery (vol. 3, pp. 238-61).

Wood, Peter H. Black Majority: Negroes in Colinial South Carolina. New York: Alfred A. Knopf, 1974. CC, CCPL, CLS, SCHS

A study of blacks and slavery in the colony from 1670 to 1740, with much information on black contributions to the colonial economy and the survival of African cultural and linguistic elements.

Yerbury, F.R. Georgian Details of Domestic Architecture. London: Ernest Benn, 1926. CLS

Consists of photographs of doorways, windows, ironwork, interior woodwork, stairs, fireplaces, etc., in 18th-century English houses. Useful for comparison with Drayton Hall details.

MAGAZINES AND JOURNALS

"American Literature and Charleston Society." Review of Anglo-American Literature and Manners, by Philarete Chasles in Southern Quarterly Review, new series, 7 (April 1853): 380-421. CC, CCPL, CLS, SCHS

Figure 19: Brickwork, 1976. Bricks for Drayton Hall were probably made locally and Flemish bond is used throughout the exterior walls of the house. (Charles E. Chase photograph, NTHP)

Figure 20: River facade, 1973. (Louis Schwartz photograph)

The author digresses from his review to contrast the lack of sociability in "modern" Charleston with the conviviality of yesteryear (pp. 402-21).

"Charleston, S.C., in 1774, As Described by an English Traveller." The Historical Magazine 9 (November 1865): 341-47. CC, CLS, SCHS

Comments on appearance of the city and its inhabitants, climate, transportation, prices for food and drink.

Cotton, Charles Caleb. "The Letters of Charles Caleb Cotton, 1798-1802." South Carolina Historical and Genealogical Magazine 51 (July and October 1950): 132-44, 216-28; 52 (January 1951): 17-25. CC, CCPL, CLS, SCHS

Letters by an English schoolmaster in Charleston. Mentions of fashions, gardens, climate, food, politics, education in South Carolina.

Dillwyn, William. "Diary of William Dillwyn during a Visit to Charles Town in 1772." Edited by A.S. Salley. South Carolina Historical and Genealogical Magazine 36 (1935): 1-6, 29-35, 73-78, 107-10. CC, CCPL, CLS, SCHS

Points of interest in the town (p. 6); "Annual Ball for Children" (p.73); deer hunt on a plantation (p. 77); description of Broom Hall and Crowfield plantations (Goose Creek area) (pp. 109-10).

Heyward, Du Bose. "Charleston: Where Mellow Past and Present Meet." National Geographic, March 1939, pp. 273-312. CC, CCPL, CLS, SCHS

Highlights of the history of the city, a tour of historic and modern sites and the gardens. By a noted Charleston author.

Howells, W[illiams] D[ean]. "In Charleston." Harper's Monthly Magazine, (October 1915): 747-57. CC, CLS

Impressions of the city early in the 20th century: buildings, society, "temperament," black population.

Lewisohn, Ludwig. "South Carolina: A Lingering Fragrance." The Nation, 12 July 1922, pp. 36-38. CC, CLS, SCHS

Contrasts old Charleston culture with the attitude of the up-country leaders who began to dominate the state in the 1890s. The author praises the former and deplores the latter.

Mechlin, Leila. "A Glimpse of Old Charleston and the Nearby Rice Plantation." American Magazine of Art 14 (September 1923): 475-85. SCHS

Refers to the sale of many plantations to Northerners as hunting preserves.

II. MAGAZINES AND JOURNALS

Ralph, Julian. "Charleston and the Carolinas." Harper's New Monthly Magazine (January 1895): 204-26. CC, CLS, SCHS

Impressions of Charleston: appearance of city, social life, clubs, charities, churches and commerce. (Phosphate mining was keeping alive the economy of the Charleston area.) (pp. 204-14)

[Rogers, Charles Kaufman.] "Beleaguered Charleston: Letters from the City, 1860-64." Edited by Martin Abbott and Elmer L. Puryear. South Carolina Historical Magazine 61 (April, July, October 1960): 61-74, 164-75, 210-18. CC, CCPL, CLS, SCHS

News of everyday life in Charleston during the War Between the States: hardships, supply problems, high prices, etc.

Rutledge, Anna Wells. "After the Cloth was Removed." Winterthur Portfolio 4 (1968): 47-62. CLS, SCHS

An examination of an 18th-century drawing of a Charleston party of the period, with descriptions of tableware and furnishings.

Sanders, Samuel D. " 'If Fortune Should Fail'; Civil War Letters of Dr. Samuel D. Sanders." Edited by Walter Rundell. South Carolina Historical Magazine 65 (July and October 1964): 129-44, 218-32. CC, CCPL, CLS, SCHS

Letters of a well-educated Confederate soldier to his daughter in Cheraw, S.C. Many of these letters were written from Morris Island near Charleston.

Sass, Herbert Ravenel. "South Carolina Rediscovered." National Geographic, March 1953, pp. 281-321. CC, CCPL, CLS, SCHS

Heavy emphasis on the Charleston area; also covers other parts of the state.

[Simms, William Gilmore.] "Charleston, the Palmetto City." Harper's New Monthly Magazine (June 1857): 1-22. CC, CLS, SCHS

Describes buildings and public institutions in the city.

Simons, Albert. "40 Years of Preservation." Preservation Progress 5 (May 1960); reprinted in Journal of the American Institute of Architects, December 1960. CCPL, CLS

Deals with the history of historic preservation efforts in the city of Charleston.

Wescoat, Arthur Brailsford. "Journal of Arthur Brailsford Wescoat, 1863-1864." South Carolina Historical Magazine 55 (April 1954): 71-102. CC, CCPL, CLS, SCHS

Diary of a schoolboy in the low country giving news from the war, local occurrences, etc.

Whitehead, Russell F., ed. <u>The Monograph Series: Recording the Architecture of the American Colonies and the Early Republic</u> 14 (1928) Nos. 2-6. CC

Discussion of Charleston buildings.